CHICAGO STREET COP

CHICAGO STREET COP

Amazing True Stories from the
Mean Streets of Chicago and Beyond

Pat McCarthy

Pat McCarthy Productions, Inc.

Pat McCarthy Productions, Inc.
Chicago, Illinois
United States of America

This is a true account. The incidents portrayed are all based on actual events I was personally involved in. A few are composites. Most names are accurate, but a few names and certain other identifying characteristics have been changed.

ISBN-13: 978-0-9966666-0-2
LCCN: 2015918483

Distributed by Itasca Books

Cover Design by Lois Stanfield
Typeset by MK Ross

Printed in the United States of America

In Dedication to my father, Detective Harry W. McCarthy,
who was a very loving father and an inspiration,
and also to my wonderful son, Officer Ryan McCarthy,
who carries on a long and proud family tradition
as a fourth generation Chicago Cop.

CONTENTS

PROLOGUE

Most people think their lives and careers should be a book. And perhaps they should. However, my life as both a Chicago street cop and working undercover for the FBI is the kind of thing you just can't make up. I knew at the time I was living through it all that I would eventually tell my story.

Growing up as a skinny Irish kid in 1950s Chicago, I had always wanted to be a cop, but not just any cop—a Chicago cop like my dad and my great-grandfather. Being a cop was almost all I ever thought and talked about. Some of my earliest memories were of watching my dad put on his Chicago Police uniform and strap on his gun belt. I watched my dad head out the door and drive away in his powder blue 1959 Chevy Bellaire to work the mean streets of Chicago and wondered what kind of excitement he would experience during his tour of duty that day. What wild and crazy things would he witness? Who were the people that my dad was going to help? People he didn't even know, but his help was of utmost importance to them at critical times in their lives.

Besides being a Chicago cop, my father, Harry, always worked side jobs in security to bring in extra money. My mother, Therese, worked part time as a waitress. We were a solid middle-class American family. Both my parents worked hard to provide for our family, in part so their kids could attend private Catholic school, and that cost big money—especially with seven kids enrolled in Catholic schools at the same time.

The Chicago neighborhood where I grew up was blue-collar, working-class families all the way—about two miles from Wrigley Field, the home of the Chicago Cubs baseball team. Most of the people in my neighborhood had normal "everyday" jobs, such as bus drivers, construction workers, cops, or firefighters. Although I was raised in an Irish Catholic family, I had many friends from diverse ethnic backgrounds.

Back in the late 1950s and even into the 60s, TV shows like *My Friend Flicka*, *Roy Rogers*, and other Wild West shows were popular at the time. While most kids played cowboys and Indians, I played cops and robbers, good guys versus bad guys. I knew that the days of becoming a cowboy were long over, but being a cop was a dream I could achieve.

≈≈≈≈≈

Most people in my middle-class neighborhood on the north side of Chicago didn't have air conditioning in their houses or apartments when I was young. On hot summer days and nights, all of the windows in their houses were wide open with screens to keep the bugs out. One sweltering night when I was just thirteen, my two brothers, four sisters, and I were watching the black-and-white TV in our front room. We heard the sound of a woman screaming loudly, as if being viciously attacked and needing help. My siblings and I jumped up and ran to look out the front window to see what was going on outside in the street. At first, I couldn't tell where the woman's piercing screams were coming from, but they seemed to be getting much louder and more intense.

Due to the extreme summer heat, I was dressed only in my underwear and a white cotton T-shirt. As I ran outside to the porch, I told my older sister Eileen to hurry up and call the police for help. As I stood barefoot on my front porch, listening to the screaming woman, it didn't take long to determine they were coming from the house almost directly across the street. Without thinking, I ran over there and up the front stairs of the house the screams were coming from. The front door was wide open, revealing a closed screen door. As I looked through the screen door, I could see a woman, who looked to be about thirty, being slapped around by a man around the same age. I opened the unlocked screen door and stepped quickly into my neighbor's front room. It didn't dawn on me at the time how silly I must have looked: a skinny thirteen-year-old kid, barging into a neighbor's house in his underwear, T-shirt, and bare feet, attempting to break up a drunken domestic disturbance.

I yelled, "Leave her alone! The police are on the way!"

The drunken batterer gave me a stunned look of amazement as he staggered backward and yelled back, "Who the fuck are you, and what are you doing in my fucking house?"

The battered wife just stared at me as if I were some space alien who had just gotten out of a space ship. I stood there, wide-eyed and stunned, looking at both of them and not knowing what to say or do. When I think back on that moment, it seemed as if the scene happened in slow motion.

Luckily, other neighbors started to gather in front of the house due to the yelling and screaming. Police cars started pulling up in front of the house, none too soon. Two uniformed officers ran into the house with guns drawn, not knowing what they might encounter.

Right away the wife cried, "Everything is all right; we were just having a little argument."

Frozen like a statue, I took it all in. The cops searched the husband right away and then sat him down on the couch. Other police officers began arriving on the scene.

The older cop who had just arrived looked at me and asked, "And who are you?"

"I live across the street. I heard a lady screaming and ran over to see what was going on."

The cop smiled and said, "Good job, kid. We'll take it from here; you can go back home now."

As I left my neighbor's house, I had to walk past the small group of neighbors gathered in front of the house to see what was going on. I walked awkwardly, but proudly, back across the street to my house, feeling like I had just done something special, regardless of my lack of clothing. I was too pumped up to feel embarrassed; adrenalin was running full speed and I was excited about what had just happened.

I'd just had my first real taste of the excitement of police work on a very small scale, and I really loved it. I don't know what I would have done if the police hadn't arrived when they did, but it was probably something that would've caused me to get my ass kicked by the drunken husband. As I walked up the front stairs of my house, my brothers and sisters were all laughing and pointing at me. But I didn't care one bit. It felt great, like I'd just experienced an amazing adventure. It would be many years before I tasted police work again, but I knew in my heart that someday I would. I really believed that it was my destiny to be a Chicago cop. In my mind, it was my calling in life.

Chapter 1

BEING A COP

I stared intensely into my bathroom mirror, shocked and somewhat surprised by the reflection staring back at me. I thought to myself, *This shit is crazy, man. How did I end up dressed up like this, and how far am I willing to go?*

I checked my makeup and lipstick one last time, just to make sure I looked good. (I did.) I slid my chrome-plated .38 caliber snub-nosed revolver into my shoulder holster, put on my fake fur coat, grabbed my purse, and quickly left my house, hoping nobody would notice me quickly walking to my car. As I pulled away from the curb, I wondered what my neighbors would think if they saw me dressed like this: a whore, a two-bit prostitute getting ready to work the streets of Chicago.

Normal men weren't supposed to dress like this, right? Normal men weren't supposed to hit the streets of any city to negotiate sex acts for money. I had to admit that nothing about what I was getting ready to do could be considered normal. Never in a million years did I think I would find myself acting as a female prostitute decoy in undercover sting operations for the Chicago Police Department (CPD). It certainly wasn't anything I ever saw my father or his cop friends do. When I first told my girlfriend Gail that I was going to be a female prostitute decoy, she gave me a strange look and said, "Pat, I always knew that you were a bit crazy, but this shit is insane." This is how it began.

The year was 1979 and I'd been in the CPD for a number

of years; currently, I was in the Special Operations Unit of the force, the unit responsible for curbing gang violence and other violent street crimes. One day, the entire Special Operations Unit was called down to the Police Academy for what was being called a "super secret" meeting about a new special operation. Everyone in the unit was abuzz with gossip and rumors. In Special Operations, it could be almost anything. We were directed to the bleachers in the Academy gym and given a speech by the deputy chief of Special Operations.

"I know I can always count on you guys for the toughest assignments. You've always been there for me, no matter what I've asked you to do. You're the best and most motivated police officers in the department. I've never put a challenge in front of you guys that you weren't able to handle. I really need some help on this; I need some volunteers for an upcoming unique and very secret operation," said Deputy Chief Charlie Pep.

One of the older veteran officers in the unit raised his hand and asked, "What is this secret assignment, boss?"

The deputy chief answered coyly, "I can't tell you just yet."

When the deputy chief said this, everyone started murmuring and became very suspicious about volunteering. They knew that if it were a good assignment, the bosses would have just assigned their favorite lackeys. I was young and dumb at the time, and an ex-marine. I knew better than to volunteer for anything, but like a jag-off, I did anyway. After the deputy chief pleaded with us for our help, I, along with several other officers, raised our hands and volunteered for the operation.

The deputy chief motioned for us to come down next to him by the podium. As we stood next to him, he shook all of our hands and said, "I knew I could count on you guys! Thanks for volunteering. Here's the plan: you guys are going to dress as female prostitute decoys and work a brand-new detail called 'operation angel.'"

Once the deputy chief made this announcement, the room turned into total chaos; many of the officers were laughing, hooting, and howling as the ten of us volunteers ran back to the bleachers.

Pep yelled over the chaos, "Calm down, you guys. This is a serious assignment, and I really need your help to make this a successful operation. The prostitution problem in many areas of the city has gotten out of control. The pimps are regularly beating up prostitutes, and the johns are also getting beaten up and robbed. The bosses downtown wanted me to put something together to stop this bullshit on the streets of Chicago. I promised them my team could handle it."

The other volunteers and I returned to the podium amid catcalls and laughter. I knew I was on my way to another great and exciting police adventure. I have always had a great desire to work undercover, but this was not exactly what I had in mind.

Pep explained, "The male officers are going to be teamed up with female officers, who will be doing most of the actual work. Basically, you guys are going to serve as bodyguards for the female police officers dressed as street prostitutes. I'm going to break you up into groups, and a sergeant will give you your assigned areas. You're going to start next weekend."

We were given several days to prepare and were also told that if we needed any help with make up or how to dress for this assignment we would be helped by a group of female officers assigned to the detail.

Back then the CPD didn't have as many females on the force as it does now. The department was reluctant to send female officers out alone to work as prostitute decoys, so they hatched a plan to send male officers dressed as a females to act as backup and to assist the female officers. Today, the female officers do as much, and sometimes more, than the men do. Times have changed.

After the initial shock wore off, we got into it and had a lot of fun preparing to hit the streets as female-prostitute decoys. When I first told my sister Eileen and my mom, they both looked at me in total disbelief. I explained, "I volunteered for this decoy assignment, and I need your help to turn me into a believable female prostitute."

Eileen finally said, "Mom, I think he's really serious about this."

Eileen was a hairdresser at the time and said, "I have a few wigs you can try on that will probably work."

My mom added, "And I have that fake fur coat you can use." They both got into it and after trying on several different outfits and makeup looks, I was ready to hit the street.

On the first night, we met at the Police Academy and were broken up into teams and assigned to our designated areas. I got lucky and was assigned to work with Janine Warner, a bright, attractive female officer, in the north side of the city.

As we headed out to our assigned areas, the energy level was high. Janine and I also had a great group of backup officers to make the arrests and transport the johns (prostitutes' customers).

Janine would approach a car that had pulled over, lean in, and ask, "What's up?"

The johns would check Janine out and couldn't wait to ask her, "How much?'

She would then say, "What do you want me to do for you?"

The johns usually responded with, "A blow job and a fuck."

Janine would then signal our backup team by running her hand through her hair; the backup team would quickly move in and make the arrest. The john would then be transported to a staging area only a mile or so away, where the arrest report would be completed. While the backup team transported the prisoner, Janine and I were instructed to stay off the street until our backup returned and set up to cover us again.

When we set up to work an area, our backup team got into a position where they could watch us without being spotted by potential customers. Janine did most of the upfront work, though: talking to the men who stopped their cars, trying to cut a sex-for-money deal. I always stood several feet behind her, attempting to hide the fact that I was a guy. The scariest times during the operation, for me, were when Janine was talking to a potential john and he would tell her that he'd rather "date" me than her. It was creepy to listen to Janine explain,

"My girlfriend is waiting for one of her regular customers to pull up any minute."

For the most part, things went smoothly and the potential johns dropped like flies. Sending Janine out on the stroll almost felt like entrapment, because the real street hookers in Chicago were weathered and often dirty and disheveled hardcore drug addicts. Janine, on the other hand, was clean-cut and pretty. I saw guys screech on their brakes when they spotted Janine walking the street as a prostitute. They would circle the block like a fish checking out a lure trolling through the water. Her good looks, blonde hair, and confident stroll were too much for many customers to resist.

Even when we arrested a potential john, he would tell us, "I knew she looked too good to be a hooker; I should have trusted my instincts." But they bit on the decoy bait anyway. The operation was like shooting fish in a barrel; the johns kept coming and our backup kept arresting them.

When I was assigned to work "operation angel," I wanted to be as prepared as possible in case I got involved in a physical altercation. I always found it odd that the police department issued batons or nightsticks for our protection, but when an officer had to hit someone with it in self-defense, everybody acted as if he'd done something wrong. I found myself in many dangerous situations over the years, in which I had to use force to protect my partner or myself. Most of the time, I used my metal flashlight, because it was a tool I carried with me day or night. On "operation angel," though, I couldn't carry my baton or metal flashlight, so I had to improvise by stashing a small can of baked beans wrapped in a towel in my purse, just in case I needed a weapon.

I never believed there were fair fights in the street; most cops don't, because no one signs up to be police officer to be beat up or hurt by anyone. The reality is there is no nice or easy way to subdue a non-compliant or combative subject. Sadly, too many officers are injured every single day, just doing their jobs in their cities or towns. If someone wanted to fight with my partner and me, any object I could use for protection was fair game, even a can of baked beans in a leather purse.

≈≈≈≈≈

I was glad that I planned ahead when Janine and I found ourselves in a weird situation one night on the job. We were waiting for our backup to return from transporting a prisoner for processing—huddled in the doorway of a nearby apartment building, like we always did when our backup was gone, killing time between arrests. Out of nowhere, two drunken fools walked up on us and wanted to party; I immediately tried to hide my face. I always felt uncomfortable when dressed like a woman, wearing lipstick and a bushy women's wig; anyone taking a close look could tell I was a man. Janine tried to get rid of these two drunks saying, "Hey, not tonight guys; my girlfriend's not feeling well."

The two drunks weren't buying it, and they kept persisting. One said, "You ladies are going to shut down for the night and party with us." Then the other guy grabbed me by the arm and tried to pull me out of the doorway.

I had no choice now, so I yelled, "Police! And we're not partying with anybody. You guys are going to jail." I shoved the guy who grabbed me and, as he pulled back, I started to whack him with my heavy bean-can purse.

The two drunks started to run away as I screamed, "Stop! Police!" and wildly swung my purse at them. As they fled, I, like a fool, gave chase and continued to whack the shit out of them as they ran into the street. These two guys literally didn't know what had hit them (a can of baked beans). They went from thinking they were going to party with two prostitutes, to getting the shit knocked out of them with a very lethal purse. My backup team arrived on the scene, just in time, as I chased these two idiots into the street.

When they spotted the unmarked squad car, they frantically started to flag them down. One guy loudly screamed, "Help us, help us! There's some crazy he-she chasing us."

My backup team got out and knocked the crap out of these two party animals for messing with us.

One backup team member yelled, "You stupid fucks! Can't you tell the difference between a real woman and a he-she?" The stunned looks on their faces were priceless.

Just another day on the job, but my life wasn't always this exciting or dramatic. I'll have to start at the beginning.

Chapter 2

THE EARLY YEARS

All my brothers and sisters attended both St. Benedict Grade School and High School in the city. I was a below-average student and somewhat of a prankster, though. By today's standards, most of the goofy shit I did to get into trouble would seem tame, but back then, especially in Catholic schools, the teaching clergy took school discipline issues seriously. In 1968, the middle of my sophomore year, the parish pastor Father Cline called me down to his office and seriously said, " Pat, you are no longer welcome at St. Bens. I have to ask you to leave and not return. I gave you several chances to straighten out, but your disruptive behavior hasn't changed."

I had to admit that I was in total shock. I protested and asked Father Cline, "What about all that 'forgive-and-forget stuff' you've preached all these years? I thought God forgives everyone."

Father Cline was clear: "Pat, I'm doing this for your own good."

So I had to leave the school and never return, making me the only one of the seven McCarthy kids not to graduate from St. Bens. I left Father Cline's office in somewhat of a daze because I couldn't believe I would no longer attend St. Bens after all these years.

When I got home I told my mom, "Father Cline threw me out of school today and told me I couldn't return." My parents were devastated and tried hard to convince Father Cline to give me another chance, but it was all in vain.

In fact, he actually told my mother, "Pat has some very serious behavioral problems and will probably end up locked up in the state prison some day." I am sure that, at the time, Father Cline could have never imagined I would spend twenty-six years of my life putting bad guys in prison as a Chicago street cop.

I always thought it was ironic that some of the best cops I knew had similar behavior problems growing up. Nothing serious, just a few misdemeanors.

My expulsion from St. Benedict High School in the middle of my sophomore year made it difficult for my parents to get me into another Catholic high school to finish out the year. After a short stint at DePaul Academy, a very strict all-boys school affiliated with De-Paul University, the home of the nationally recognized Blue Demons, the school closed its doors. I happily transferred to Amundsen High School, a co-ed public school located at Damen and Foster Avenue on the north side of Chicago.

It's ironic that because I was thrown out of St. Benedicts, I met my true love in life, Gail Tani. Gail was the most beautiful girl I had ever met. She had jet-black hair that hung down to her waist, and such a beautiful smile that it melted my heart. Her complexion was smooth and olive-colored; her almond-shaped eyes made her look exotic and sexy as hell. Even though Gail lived only about a block away from me as the crow flies, we had never met. I first noticed her at Amundsen High School when she sat directly behind me in a study hall. I imme-diately knew that I liked Gail but didn't think I had a snowball's chance in hell with her. How could she fall for a skinny Irish guy who was always fighting and acting a fool? I had a solid-D grade point average, while Gail was a straight-A student.

My assigned seat was in row two; Gail sat in row three just be-hind me and one seat to my left, which made it very easy for us to talk, which we did often. I remember one day when Gail said, "I'm going to a dance with a girlfriend at St. Benedicts this coming Saturday. Are you going?"

I still had many friends at St. Bens who regularly attended the

lice cadet, I did represent the Chicago Police Department when I met with these business owners.

It felt as if I were getting closer to realizing my dream of becoming a sworn officer, but fate was not on my side. After six months in the 18th District, I was informed that, due to budget crunches, the Police Cadet Program was being scrapped. Within a few months, the cadets would all be out of jobs; I was crushed. My career path was not going to go as smoothly as I had originally planned. I had two more years to wait until I was eligible to take the Police Academy entrance test when I turned twenty-one. After two years of bouncing around various jobs, such as a lifeguard and truck driver, I was finally old enough in 1972.

The Police Academy entrance test was being given at several different locations throughout the city that year due to the large number of applicants—6,000. I had to take the test at Lane Technical High School, a large, older school in the north side of the city. When I pulled up in front of the school, the number of people I saw stunned me. It looked as if half the people in the city were there to take the police exam. I waded through a crowd that seemed more like something you'd encounter at a professional sports game, not at a police exam. I was directed by a hall monitor through a series of massive hallways and finally located my assigned room where I was to take the test.

To be honest, I was scared to death and could feel my heart pounding wildly inside my chest. I wanted to do well on the test, but I wasn't sure I would. A room monitor stood at a podium in front of the classroom and gave me and the twenty-nine other prospective cops the testing rules: "Ladies and gentlemen, you are not allowed to leave this classroom for any reason unless it is an emergency. In addition, you cannot have any writing materials, paper, or notebooks on your desks. You have a time limit of two hours to complete the test. When you are finished with the test, place your completed test booklets on the monitor's desk and leave the school immediately. You will be notified of your results by registered mail within several weeks."

The testing began. The clock was ticking, and I had only two hours to become a cop. I opened my test booklet, took a quick look at the material, and started answering the questions. Some were simple, while others appeared to be written in a foreign language. I finished answering most of them and guessed at the remaining questions in about an hour and a half. I left the school in somewhat of a daze, trying to analyze how I might have done on the test. I really had no idea, but my past track record of taking tests in both grade school and high school gave me a sinking feeling in my stomach.

Much to my amazement, I did better than expected. The test results were broken down into three categories: well qualified, qualified, and not qualified. I was thrilled to have landed in the qualified category, and I was so pumped up and excited at having more than a decent chance of becoming a Chicago cop. Slowly, the Police Department began hiring classes of new recruits from the list I was on. If events took their normal course, I would be on the job as a Chicago street cop within a year. Well, like many things in life, it didn't come off as smoothly as I'd have liked.

In 1973, about a year after I took the police test, a group of minority test applicants filed a federal lawsuit, stating that the test was unfair and discriminated against them. Shortly after the lawsuit was filed, a federal injunction was issued that prohibited the City of Chicago from hiring anyone else from the list I was on. The hiring injunction issued by the federal court meant that a lengthy court hearing was going to take place to determine if the lawsuit had any validity to it. Federal Judge Prentice Marshall was assigned the case in Chicago's Federal District Court.

When the lawsuit was first filed, everyone expected a quick resolution. However, the federal court case dragged on for three years. Finally, in early 1976, Judge Marshall ruled that the city could hire one more recruit class from the list, then the list would be eliminated, and a new entrance test had to be developed. I was one of the lucky recruits in that last class. On April 15, 1976, I received my official acceptance letter by registered mail to start recruit training. Tears streamed down my face as I read that I was to report to the Chicago Police Academy on April 26. In ten days, I would officially become a probationary police officer in the Chicago Police Department. Over the next several days, I felt like I was walking on a cloud; it had been six long years since I'd first become a CPD cadet.

Chapter 3

THE POLICE ACADEMY

The night before my first day at the Academy, Gail wanted to celebrate by throwing a surprise BBQ for many of my friends and family. She said, "I know how much this means to you, Pat, and it deserves a special party." Everybody knew I had always wanted to be a cop, and that tomorrow was going to be a great day in my life. Many of my close friends and family members said such nice things that it made me realize how truly lucky I was.

A very dear friend, Timmy Ryan, gave me a big bear hug and said, "Who says dreams don't come true?"

Timmy knew how much I wanted to be a Chicago cop like my dad, and I was completely blown away. With tears welling up in my eyes I told him, "This really is a dream come true for me, and I know how lucky I am. Thanks, bro."

That night I had a hard time sleeping; the anticipation and excitement were almost overwhelming. I was only hours away from becoming a third-generation Chicago cop and being part of a proud heritage, a family legacy. As my mind raced, I had visions of the excitement that awaited me: lights, sirens, high-speed car chases, and shootouts. I couldn't wait to get started on my career. That night was one of the longest nights in my life.

It took about forty-five minutes to drive to the Police Academy, which was located at 720 W. O'Brien, to begin my six months of police training. It was the same building I had worked in earlier as a CPD cadet. The Police Academy was one of the oldest buildings in the city and it was pretty rundown, but to me it looked like a palace where great things were about to happen. As I parked my car and walked toward my future, I was the happiest and most excited I had ever been. My lifelong hopes and dreams about being a Chicago cop were finally going to be realized.

As I entered, I was directed to a classroom with around thirty other recruits. My class actually consisted of ninety recruits but we were divided into three separate homerooms. Each homeroom had a sergeant who was the class commander. My homeroom sergeant was Sergeant Glass, a very classy and distinguished-looking African-American police officer. He was a great guy, who was always smiling and made everyone around him feel comfortable.

Sergeant Glass said, "You are now held to a higher standard. You are joining an elite fraternity and are now probationary police officers for the Chicago Police Department." He then laid down the law about the Academy rules and regulations. We were given a dress code (probationary police officers attending the Police Academy are required to wear tan khaki pants and tan shirts) and a code of conduct that was to be strictly followed and maintained throughout our training. Glass added, "You will be subject to daily uniform inspections and you'd better be squared away, which means shoes shined, shirts clean and pressed, and pants creased." We were not allowed to wear official police department uniforms until the final few weeks of training. I took it all in, but I couldn't wait to get to the classes that talked about real police work.

The nuts and bolts of the job were only a few weeks away and when it finally started, I was enthralled. I hung on the instructors' every word. I took my training books home at night and read them over and over; I couldn't get enough information about real police work. We were given a wide variety of instruction on many different law-enforcement topics. Most citizens don't realize the complex training police officers receive as they progress through the Academy. The awesome authority and responsibility to be able to handle the most high-stress situations and violent circumstances outside of an active war zone are repeated over and over again.

Role-playing is a big part of the training, but hitting a probationary officer with a rolled-up newspaper and yelling and swearing at them is not even close to the reality of the street. Everyone knew the worst that could happen to a cadet in the Academy was a sprained arm or ankle. Similar incidents on the street are far more lethal and often end in police officers being killed or seriously injured. The authority to use deadly force is taken extremely seriously by everyone. Police officers have to respond to some of the most violent and dangerous situations any man or woman could possibly face.

Police officers are expected to act like robots without feelings and emotion. Academy training can only marginally prepare officers for the very real situations they will face in their careers; the real-world training takes place in stench-filled bars and ghetto neighborhoods. The Chicago Police Department's rules and regulations are known as General Orders, which outline the conduct expected of all officers in almost any situation they might face—not only on duty, but the expected conduct of off-duty officers. The department also had what is known as Special Orders, which cover any unique situations that may not be fully covered in the department's General Orders. Legal issues related to police work were also covered in depth.

We were also told that the news media is not a cop's friend. Newspaper and television reporters often slant many of their stories to make the police look bad. They tend to give the false impression that cops are gunning down unarmed innocent civilians at an alarming rate. The saying in the news media is, "If it bleeds, it leads." The facts are that police officers all across this country—in both big cities and small towns—experience violent encounters on a daily basis with some of the most dangerous animals/people on this planet. The real truth is that less that 1% of these violent encounters result in an officer using deadly force. The real truth is that nearly all police officers use great restraint in the use of deadly force. However, there are some bad cops out there, and they are giving the rest of us a bad name.

For example, the Department of Justice (DOJ) released an eighty-seven-page report after sending twenty FBI Special Agents to Ferguson, Missouri, to work full time on the Ferguson investigation. I worked with Feds for eleven years and have never seen this type of scrutiny before on any other case. Their extensive investigation revealed the truth: the witnesses who said that Michael Brown had his hands up and was surrendering were proved to be complete liars. Unfortunately, the investigation also revealed some systemic bigotry in that force, which is proving to be a large part of the image problem. But back to life at the Police Academy.

The classes we attended on various legal issues were usually taught to us by instructors who were lawyers from the city's legal department; some instructors were police officers with law school backgrounds. We also received extensive information on first aid, such as how to treat people in shock or how to stop the bleeding from a knife or gunshot wound. These were skills that most other police officers and I sadly have had to use many times over our careers.

Physical fitness training was also a major part of the Academy's training regiment. We had to learn to take down unruly alcohol- and drug-fueled criminals who fought very hard to get away so they wouldn't have to go to jail. We also ran three miles every day and worked out in the gym, lifting weights and learning take down moves and handcuffing techniques. Captain Harold Brown, an ex-marine who was an intense and no-nonsense cop, was in charge of physical training. His right-hand man was a tough-as-nails sergeant named Stanley Sarbaneck, who was known for his rough handling of new recruits when they were being taught various defensive tactics. Police work has many perils, and one of the most dangerous is trying to control and subdue a buzzed-up asshole who would do almost anything to stay out of jail. Many legendary stories of recruits sustaining broken arms and fractured wrists during physical training still exist.

The Academy also had instructional blocks of training, in which police officers from many different units within the CPD came to describe the functions of their specialized units and what resources were available to all cops. We were also lectured on how to be a "beat cop." (Beat cops are the police officers citizens see patrolling a city or town in uniform in marked squad cars.)

In some areas of the country, patrol officers can assist these various specialized units. One of the police instructors who blew me away was a young Hispanic cop from the Narcotics Unit. He was a great guy with a good personality and a real love for the job that showed in his presentation. He gave a talk on the function of the Narcotics Unit. He also told some personal stories about his undercover work as a narcotics cop.

He said, "Narcotics work takes a special skill set, and not every officer is cut out for the stress, nor do they all have the ability to playact in the intense situations they have to deal with." He went on to tell us about a case he worked on: "I was alone in an apartment with three hardcore drug dealers, when one of the dealers accused me of being a cop. I played it off and everything went well, but I knew they were watching me closely for any sign of nervousness or fear. I turned the situation back on them by accusing the dealers of being too paranoid from using too much dope. But this doesn't come naturally; you have to be focused and ready for anything because your life is always on the line."

You could hear a pin drop in the room while he related his undercover experiences. If it were God himself talking to us, I couldn't have been more impressed. I hung on his every word. When he finished his presentation, he hung around and shot the shit with a group of us from the class about undercover narcotics work. I knew right then and there that someday, somehow, I would work undercover. Never could I have imagined on that day in the Academy, sitting there as a recruit, that I would spend five exciting years of my life as an undercover cop in the Gang Crimes Unit, buying guns and drugs from hardcore street-gang members. My life was on the line every day and any little slipup could have meant the end.

My time at the Academy was typical. It was something we all had to get through before we could hit the streets to patrol as real street cops. The time dragged on, but the big day in our training finally arrived, and it was a memorable one.

≈≈≈≈≈

My recruit class was given our police badges and the shields for our uniform hats at a ceremony held at the Academy in August of 1976. It was an extremely emotional day for me for several reasons. I would continue a long and proud family tradition that started back in the late 1800s with my great-grandfather. But what really made this an emotional day for me was that the Chicago Police Department badge # 15827 I received at the ceremony was the former badge of my best friend, Mike Begley. Mike and I grew up just one block away from each other and, as kids, we were inseparable.

Like me, Mike had always wanted to be a Chicago cop, and it was something important that we had in common. Like my father, Mike's dad also was a Chicago cop. We truly were as close as brothers. Mike also joined the Marine Corps right out of high school, but he wasn't a weekend warrior like me. He joined for a full two-year tour of duty, was sent to Vietnam after boot camp, and spent a tough year there. When he returned, he took the test with me and was hired just before Judge Marshall instituted the three-year hiring freeze.

Mike had just completed most of his Academy training in 1972 and was temporarily assigned to work uniformed patrol in the 20th District – Foster Avenue, a quiet station on the north side of the city. After graduating from the Police Academy, officers are still on probation until one year from their starting dates. Mike was working as a probationary beat cop and, like me, he also loved to ride motorcycles. He had recently bought a Triumph motorcycle from a fellow cop who was in the process of getting a divorce and gave Mike a great deal on the bike. He loved his motorcycle and rode it often.

Tragically, on March 31, 1972, he was cruising the neighborhood on his day off when a woman blew through a stop sign at the intersection of Irving Park Road and Oakley and ran broadside into Mike. Unfortunately, Mike wasn't wearing a motorcycle helmet and sustained massive injuries to his right leg and his head. A fire department ambulance rushed him to Ravenswood Hospital about two miles from the accident site, and he died on the operating room table a short time later during brain surgery. I lost my best friend that day; it was one of the saddest days of my life.

After Mike died, I kept in touch with his family. When I entered the Police Academy, Mike's dad gave me a box containing Mike's gun, police wallet, belts, and holster. He told me that Mike would have wanted me to have them. I couldn't help but think how unfair it was that Mike's dreams had been cut so short and that he had died so young. It really made me realize at a young age how true that the saying, "Life is a gift; live everyday to its fullest," really is—especially for cops.

The day we were presented our police badges at the police academy was the best day of the entire process of becoming police officers. We were officially sworn in and could now wear the Chicago Police Department uniform. The only way anyone could tell we were brand-new recruits was by the newness of our leather gun belts and holsters. I was the only recruit in my class who had equipment with some real wear on it. Wearing Mike's gun belt and holster and carrying his badge meant so much to me. I felt a deep emotional closeness to Mike that I hadn't felt in a very long time. I made a promise to Mike that day that I would carry on with our dream, sadly, without him. Mike would be with me in spirit throughout my police career every step of the way. I carried Mike's wallet every day as a cop, except for the five years that I worked undercover in the Gang Crimes Unit. I still have Mike's police equipment today.

Even though my recruit class still had several weeks of training left before graduation, the atmosphere at the Police Academy changed instantly. My classmates looked and acted different; you could see the air of authority in their faces and the way they carried themselves. They seemed to walk a little taller, a little straighter. With only a few days of training left, everyone was getting restless. We anxiously awaited our new assignments. The anticipation was intense, as no one knew which of the twenty-five police districts scattered throughout the city we would be assigned to.

The big day for my recruit class finally arrived. Sergeant Glass stood in front of my class and read our new assignments. Mine was the 12th District – Monroe, located just south and west of downtown Chicago. I was totally stunned, because CPD usually assigned officers from the south side of Chicago to south-side districts and north-side officers to north-side districts. I was a "north-sider," but I couldn't have been happier with my new assignment. The ethnic makeup of the 12th District was mostly African-American and Hispanic, with a small Italian section known as Little Italy. It was considered a high-crime district and exactly the type of police district I wanted to work in. I couldn't wait to get started working the street.

Later that same day, my recruit class took our daily three-mile run on the city streets near the Police Academy. As we were running in formation, I noticed an unmarked dark-maroon Dodge police car slowly driving by. I took a closer look at the unmarked squad car and realized that my dad was driving. My father, Harry, was an undercover detective with the Subterfuge Unit of the Vice Control Division. The Subterfuge Unit worked undercover operations in many areas of the vice trade throughout the city, including prostitution, gambling, and illegal sales of alcohol and cigarettes. His boss was Commander Mike O'Donnell, who had been my dad's best friend ever since they were young kids growing up together on the west side of Chicago.

The Vice Unit headquarters was located at 943 W. Maxwell Street, only a few short blocks away from the Police Academy. It was also the building featured in the opening montage of the 1970s hit TV series, *Hill Street*

Blues, a popular cop show that revolved around the lives and the careers of the police officers who worked at that station—even though the series was set in Boston. I broke from the formation and ran into the street, flagging down my dad. I was very excited and couldn't wait to tell him the good news about my new assignment to the 12th District. He pulled over and the surprised look on my dad's face said it all; he wasn't happy.

I remember my dad's exact response to my news: "Oh, shit! I should have made a call."

But I said, "Dad, I'm so glad you didn't. I want to work in a place like the 12th. This district has a good mix of many aspects of crime: it's got the projects, skid row on Madison Street, Little Italy on Taylor Street with organized crime (the Mafia), and 18th Street with a major concentration of Mexican gangs. I'll learn a lot about police work here."

His reply was instant: "Pat, I don't want you dealing with crazy shit every day. The job is different now than it used to be; people are much more violent, even toward cops. It's just too dangerous."

"I'll be okay, Dad. I promise. This is what I want." I leaned into my father's undercover car and gave him a kiss on the cheek. "I love ya, Pop. I'll be fine."

I then ran really fast to catch up to my Academy classmates. I have to admit that my dad's negative reaction only reinforced the excited feeling I had about my new assignment to the ghetto. I knew that I would experience the kind of action I became a cop to experience.

My dad had many high-ranking friends in CPD. With a phone call to one of his friends on the job, he might have been able to get me assigned to a less active north-side district, although I'm truly glad he didn't. My dad and I had many spirited conversations over the years about police work; many occurred even before I was an officer.

He knew I was a little reckless at times, and he would always try to warn me: "Never be the first cop through the door on calls." My dad explained, "Pat, when shit turns bad on a call, it's usually the first cop through the door who gets shot."

I was always a little cocky as a kid growing up, and my dad worried that my cockiness would get me hurt on the street. I distinctly remember one serious conversation we had. My dad looked me straight in the eye and said, "Please, Pat, never go in first. Let other cops take the lead."

I said, "I'm sorry, Pop, but I don't work like that. I *want* to be the first one in on calls." My dad was frustrated with me because I was so reckless and cocky. I feel bad now that my cockiness caused my dad stress he shouldn't have had to deal with, but I was serious. I joined the CPD to be a good police officer. That's just how I felt.

Chapter 4

GOING TO THE GHETTO

The 12th District – Monroe is located at 100 S. Racine Street and was one of the oldest police stations in Chicago. The police department has three different shifts to cover a twenty-four-hour day—referred to as days, afternoons, and midnights. I called the district secretary to get my watch assignment, which was, unsurprisingly, the midnight shift. I would be working from midnight to 8:00 a.m.—the graveyard shift, as it is referred to in police circles. Cops assigned to work the midnight shift either loved it or hated it. Your whole life is thrown into complete turmoil: While the rest of the world sleeps, you are working. While you are at home sleeping, the normal world is working.

As one veteran cop said to me once, "There aren't too many legit people out on the street after midnight." *How right he was, and I would soon learn what that cop told me was the unfiltered truth.*

As I parked my personal car in front of the 12th District station, I felt ready and excited to start my first shift. I was really surprised by how small the building actually was. It was a narrow, two-story brick building with a small parking lot next to it. The parking lot couldn't hold all the district's squad cars, so they were parked all over the place: on the nearby streets, even on the sidewalk next to the station. As I entered the station, I was surprised to see a homeless guy passed out on the small stairway leading to the inside of the station house. As I climbed the well-worn stairs, I couldn't help but wonder why they would let this street bum sleep in such an important place as a police station. As crazy as it may sound, the station cops knew many of the drunken piss bums by name and had compassion for them. The officers who worked at the 12th District often gave them a few bucks and a baloney sandwich from the station's lock-up; it's what prisoners were served while they were in custody and awaiting a court appearance. The 12th District actually had a small courtroom on the second floor down the hall from the roll-call room. The bums were allowed to pass out in the station's stairway and catch some sleep away from the outside element—as long as they slept to the side, so cops and citizens could walk past them. I know it probably sounds odd, but that's just how it was; things are different in the ghetto.

Once inside, I was again surprised by how small the interior of the police station was. Cops were walking around everywhere: seasoned street cops, wearing well-worn leather belts and holsters, not rookies like me. I was immediately impressed. I felt like Christopher Columbus discovering a brand new continent. I wanted to take it all in, the sights, the sounds, the smells. The front desk was about chest high. I could hear the sound of police radios squawking all around me. I approached the front desk and told a uniformed cop that I was reporting in to work the midnight shift.

The cop barely acknowledged me as he yelled out, "Sarge, we got another rookie reporting in."

The desk sergeant approached, shook my hand, and said, "Welcome aboard, kid. You're a little early, but roll call is up those stairs." He pointed me in the direction of a narrow stairway leading to the second floor.

I said, "Thank you, sir," and headed up the well-worn stairs to my first official roll call as a Chicago cop. I thought, *How many other rookie police officers have walked these same stairs over the years?* I'm sure they had the same anxious but excited feelings as mine: the feeling of uncertainty, the fear of the unknown, and the nagging feeling in my gut as I wondered, *Am I up to the serious challenges I am about to face?*

Will I be able to handle the pure insanity of working as a street cop in the ghetto?

Only two other cops were in the roll-call room: one was sitting there reading a newspaper, the other was sleeping with his head down in his arms. The cop reading the newspaper gave me a quick glance but said nothing and immediately went back to his newspaper. The other cop remained sound asleep in his seat. I sat in awkward silence for a short time as the room slowly started to fill up in a steady flow of other officers. I recognized another recruit from the Police Academy and said, "Hey, how you doing?" while trying not to act as nervous as I felt. I gave him a nod and a wave of acknowledgement.

He waved back and seemed as nervous and as uncomfortable as I was. It wasn't long before the room began to fill up with police officers, and the atmosphere quickly changed. The room seemed to come alive as cops shot the shit with each other. I sat there taking it all in and wondering which one of these cops was going to be my field-training officer (FTO).

The watch commander, Lieutenant Don Kelly, walked into the room and stood behind the podium to begin conducting roll call. I sat erect in my chair, giving the lieutenant my full attention, but it seemed as if the other recruit and I were the only ones paying attention as he started roll call. I was surprised by how the other cops in the room barely seemed to notice and just kept bantering with each other.

Finally, the lieutenant yelled, "Hey, quiet down you guys! We have business to take care of here!" To my surprise, everyone quieted down as the lieutenant began to read off officer's names: "Johnson and Branfield, take car 1221, and pay special attention to 1209 S. Racine. We've had several shootings in and around that building the last few days." Then he made a special announcement: "I want to welcome two new rookies to the district. McCarthy and Perone, stand up please." We stood up to be acknowledged and were greeted by a polite round of applause and a few catcalls. The other recruit and I stood there red faced and embarrassed.

Lieutenant Kelly then said, "McCarthy, your field-training officer is Larry Soltysiak." Larry gave me a slight smile and polite wave. Kelly continued, "The Mexicans are going at it on 18th Street. It seems like there's an ongoing dispute between the 26ers gang and the Latin Counts. We've recently had several shootings in the area, one was a homicide. You all know that means they'll be some retaliation soon." He moved on to, "Hansen, pass out the daily bulletins and make sure that every team gets one."

The daily bulletin is a one-page sheet with wanted suspects' photos and information about their crimes on the front side. I was somewhat surprised that the pictures were mostly of male blacks who looked pretty scary. The back page listed vehicles that had recently been reported stolen in Chicago. I was shocked by how many stolen vehicles were on the back page of the daily bulletin; hundreds of license plates were listed in neat rows from the very top of the page to the very bottom.

When roll call ended, my FTO, Larry Soltysiak, approached me and said, "Hi, Pat, we're going to be spending a lot of time together, and I want it to be a good learning experience for you. I'll take it personally if you don't ask me a lot of questions." He went on to say, "I take my job seriously, and when your training session with me is over, I want you to be the best you can be."

I was immediately impressed by Larry: He was all business and you could tell just by looking at him that he was serious about being a good cop. He was in great shape physically, his uniform was impeccable, his shoes were brightly shined, hair and mustache neat and trimmed. As I checked out the other cops on my new watch, I realized how lucky I was with my assigned FTO, Larry. Most of the other cops were badly out of shape and looked disheveled in their old and wrinkled uniforms. Larry gave me a quick tour of the station house and introduced me to several coppers who worked in the district. We then picked up our radio and squad car keys and headed out into the night, a night I had been waiting for years to experience.

Larry and I were assigned to work patrol beat 1223. The 12th District was divided into beats that could consist of several miles or be as small as a few block-long areas. The beats were determined by the amount of crime that took place within certain boundaries in the district. Even when you were assigned a specific beat, you could also patrol other areas in the district and respond to calls to assist other beat officers. When we got into our patrol car, Larry walked me through the basics of how the squad car worked: He activated the lights and siren and did a general check of the vehicle inside and out. He schooled me that you should always check your squad car thoroughly before leaving the station. Larry emphasized that you always check the outside of the vehicle for any new damage. He told me stories of how some cops would get involved in a minor accident or fender bender, not report it, and hope to pass the blame on to the next cop who drove the squad car.

Larry also taught me: "Always pull out the backseat and check underneath and behind the seat for weapons that might have been discarded by suspects who sat back there during the previous shift. Bad guys often discard their weapons and dope in the backseat area of the patrol car on their way to jail so it can't be used as evidence against them. Pat, it might seem hard to believe but some lazy cop can put a suspect in the squad car without thoroughly searching them. It could cost *us* our lives if anyone we put in the back finds a discarded weapon there. It's an important officer-safety issue, and this search must be done before every shift."

I was fascinated by what Larry was teaching me; we hadn't even left the parking lot yet for my first official tour of duty and I was already learning new things about the job of being a street cop. This type of real-world street information was never discussed at the Academy. As we pulled out of the station parking lot, I finally felt like an "official" street cop; it truly was an amazing feeling. Larry drove around the district, pointing out various locations I needed to be aware of, such as where the whores hung out and known gang hot spots. The district had eight high-rise project buildings and numerous two-story low-risers, or row houses as they were called, scattered around it.

It wasn't long before we received the first radio assignment of the night: "man with a gun call on the tenth floor of 1414 West 14th Place." Larry activated the lights and siren and took off, driving like a maniac toward the projects. I was so excited that my heart was in my throat. I was lightheaded and breathing heavily as I tried to calm myself. The siren was so loud inside the car that I thought the wailing sound would pop my eardrums. I watched the blue mars lights on the roof of our squad car reflecting off the buildings and parked cars as we raced past them.

As Larry drove, he said, "Just stay close to me at all times during the call and do *exactly* what I tell you. Don't try to be a hero on your first call."

"I can assure you I have no problem with that," I responded.

When we pulled up to the building in the projects, I was shocked to see another squad car had beaten us to the call. The way Larry drove, I couldn't believe anyone could get there before we did. Two other cops from the district were just getting out of their car in front of the project building as Larry screeched to a stop behind them. I was so excited and lightheaded from the high-speed, wild ride to the call that I was afraid my legs wouldn't support my weight and they'd give out on me.

Larry, the other two cops from the district, and I walked quickly to the front entrance of the project building. Everyone seemed calm but me. When we were about twenty feet from the front door, we drew guns. Suddenly, Larry yelled, "Let's go!" and everyone took off and ran toward the building's entrance. I suddenly realized I had better run, too. Once inside the building's lobby, which seemed surprisingly small for such a tall building, one of the cops pushed the elevator's up button several times, and we waited anxiously for the elevator to arrive to take us into the untamed world of policing in a big-city project building. As we waited for the elevator to arrive, Larry introduced me to the other two beat cops from the district. I was again struck by how calm and collected they were.

My heart felt like it was beating so fast that it might explode. I tried to act as cool as possible while Larry introduced me, as if we were at some normal social function, not in a potential life-and-death police action: "Guys, this is Pat McCarthy, my new trainee."

Both cops shook my hand and said, "Welcome to the ghetto; you're in for a wild ride." At the time I didn't realize how true that statement was.

The elevator we rode was filthy with discarded food wrappers and other garbage strewn around. I had read many cop books as a kid and the cops often talked about project elevators smelling like piss. I couldn't believe some ignorant pricks would actually piss in an elevator, but they do on a regular basis. I would soon learn that every project elevator on my beat smelled exactly the same way: just like stale piss.

Larry and the other two cops chatted about everyday shit as if we were headed to a BBQ at a friend's house, not a "man with a gun" call in the projects. I'll admit I was in total shock. I knew by Larry's and the other cops' demeanors they weren't too worried, but all the time I was thinking that at any moment the elevator door would open and we would all be shot dead by some madman with a gun. When the elevator stopped on the tenth floor, the door slowly opened, and we stepped out into a long narrow hallway that had a concrete walkway with see-through steel mesh from the ground to the ceiling. I fell in step directly behind Larry like a baby cub would follow its mother through the woods, staying real close for protection. I could hear the sounds of people arguing loudly nearby

A small group of people, including several young kids, were milling around in front of one apartment doorway. One of them saw us getting off the elevator and pointed without saying a word toward the apartment where the loud argument was coming from. Larry took charge immediately and began asking, "So who called the police? And who has the gun?"

One of the teens said right away, "Ain't nobody got no gun, officer. They just arguing over some bullshit."

Larry repeated, "Then who called the police and said someone had a gun?" Everyone played stupid, and nobody would admit to making the call about a man with a gun.

We quickly searched everyone standing in the hallway for weapons before we cautiously entered the project apartment. Once inside, I was shocked by the filth. Garbage was strewn everywhere. Little kids were running around in various stages of dress, including one little girl who was completely naked and crying. A skinny male, who appeared to be in his late twenties, was arguing with a fat woman about the same age. They were both drunk and completely out of control, each one trying to out-stupid the other. It looked to me like a draw; they both were idiots.

After listening to their ignorant, drunken tirades, calling each other bitches and assholes for a few minutes, we searched the apartment and determined no gun was involved in the incident. Larry said, "Keep it down! If we have to return here again, you will both be arrested and spend the rest of the night in jail."

We left the apartment and returned to our squad car, which was parked near the entrance of the project building. I asked Larry, "How can people be so ignorant and live like that?"

Larry said what I would hear throughout my career, "Pat, you're in the ghetto now, and it's just different here; these people exist in a very violent and uncivilized world." This domestic disturbance in the projects was definitely different from the one I experienced across the street from my house on Leavitt Street as a young, naive thirteen-year-old kid many years earlier.

On the ride back down the elevator, I asked Larry, "Why did you suddenly start to run as we approached the front of the building?"

He explained, "Whenever you respond to a call in the projects, you always try to get inside the building as quickly as possible because very often when the police enter the projects, residents oftentimes will throw various items from the upper floors, trying to hit them." Larry went on, "I've seen bowling balls and other objects being dropped. Throwing bags of shit and piss at the police is also a common occurrence. One time a marked squad car was parked next to one of the project buildings, and someone dropped a bowling ball that landed on the hood of the squad car, crushing the hood and damaging the engine, putting that squad car out of commission for a long time. It's dangerous here in more ways than one."

Over the next year and a half, I would experience life in the projects as very few outsiders ever do. I learned a valuable lesson on my first call: Whenever you leave a project building, run until you're about twenty feet from the building. You may be shot at, but at least you won't get pissed or shit on.

When we got back to our squad car, I had many questions to ask Larry about what had just happened on the man with a gun call we had just left: "What about the original 'a man with a gun' call? Why would someone straight-out lie about a gun when they knew it was pure bullshit; no gun was ever in the picture? We drove like mad men, risking our safety and that of innocent citizens in our efforts to get to the call to help! What gives, Larry?"

"Often the person calling the police will say someone has a gun *just* to get the police to respond faster. Most of the gun calls we respond to are just bullshit calls. These people play fast and loose with the truth."

I asked, "And what's with all those little kids running in the project hallways so late at night? Why weren't those young kids in bed sleeping like normal kids their age?" After all, it was after 1:00 a.m. Most kids I knew would never be up that late, much less outside their homes at that hour.

Larry smiled and said, "Pat, forget about anything you ever thought of as 'normal behavior'; things are just very different in the ghetto."

Boy, was Larry ever right. I used to tell people when I first started out on the job as a young cop that when I left my home for work, it was like getting on a spaceship and traveling to another planet. That's how crazy it really was. I remember a call I responded to many months later in the same project building. Several other officers and I were waiting in the lobby for the elevator to arrive. We were responding to a "battery in progress" call, which in plain English means a fight was in progress, on one of the upper floors. Several people were also waiting for the same elevator. When the elevator arrived in the lobby, the door slowly opened and a cute little African-American girl, about four or five years old, ran into the elevator in front of us. The young girl's fat-assed mother chased after her and gave the little girl a hard, opened-handed slap right across her cute, innocent little face.

The mother then screamed at her, "Get out the elevator, nigger, and let the Po-lice on!" The mother then dragged the little girl off the elevator, giving me and the other police officers a nod and a smile, as if she'd just done something good and respectful for us.

I felt so sorry for that darling little girl. I wanted to tell that piece-of-shit mother how ignorant she was, but I sadly realized it was no use; that was probably the same way she had been raised. I thought about the sad reality that, with a mother like that as a role model, what chance did this little girl really have to grow up as a normal, functioning human being? I also realized that if this mother would abuse her child in front of the police, what kind of outrageous shit did she do to her little girl when they were alone and she was high on drugs or had too much to drink?

I really enjoyed my field-training period with Larry; it seemed like every day I learned something new about police work. After a few weeks together, Larry and I really became close. I loved his passion for the job, and I really appreciated how he took the time to explain the various aspects of the job in great detail to me. Every day was a new adventure. It was interesting, exciting, and fun work learning how to be a real street cop from a true professional.

One aspect of the job I never liked or became used to was writing traffic tickets for minor traffic violations. Larry insisted that it was part of the job, and he made sure that I wrote at least one moving-violation ticket on each tour of duty. You always hear that police officers have a ticket-writing quota they must meet. Well, in some respects, that's true. All of our activity was charted monthly, and if you didn't write enough traffic tickets during that month you would be called in and counseled by the watch commander for lack of activity. It was widely stated in police circles that any cop who works an eight-hour shift could probably write at least ten traffic tickets if they really wanted to. Larry's specialty was writing people tickets for having only one working headlight on their cars. He explained that the ticketed citizen only had to bring in a receipt to court showing that the headlight was repaired, and the traffic court judge would dismiss the charges.

Larry explained it this way, "Pat, we did our job, but we really didn't hurt anyone too badly."

I didn't really buy that logic and I hated it when Larry pulled a citizen's car over and told me to write them a ticket for the headlight violation. People would literally beg you not to write them a ticket. I heard every story in the book—from I just lost my job to my wife died yesterday. We worked in the ghetto. People had a tough enough time just getting by in life and here I was fucking with them by writing them a bullshit traffic ticket. By issuing the ticket, it meant that the citizen had to take off work to go to court and many of them probably had more important things to spend their money on than a broken car headlight. Some aspects of being a cop were a lot more complicated than I had first realized.

The time finally came when my training days with Larry were over; I learned so much in the few short months we worked together as partners. Larry was a great guy and a great cop, and to this day I'm thankful for all the wisdom and knowledge he shared with me during my training period. It was with mixed feelings that I thanked Larry for being a great field-training officer and said good-bye after our final shift together.

I couldn't believe how fast the time flew by, but my first year on the job was over. After the probationary period ended, I was assigned to a permanent watch as a full-fledged police officer. Most of the time, new officers are assigned to a different district than the one where they are initially trained. It was somewhat unusual, but I was lucky and my permanent assignment allowed me to remain in the 12th District. As I would find out later, my entire career would take many unusual paths. But for now, I couldn't have been happier about my permanent assignment. Many of my classmates from the Academy were sent to different districts. For them it would be like starting all over again, but I would stay on familiar turf in the 12th District, at least for the time being.

Chapter 5

At Home in the Ghetto

Back in those days—the 1970s and until the early '80s when the CPD got unionized and started being represented by the Fraternal Order of Police (FOP)—a cop changed shifts (also called "watches") every twenty-eight days. It was crazy: just as you started getting used to working one shift, it was time to change to the next one. One month you would be working from 11:00 p.m. until 7:00 a.m. The next month your shift would change, and you'd be working from 3:00 p.m. until 11:00 p.m. The following month you'd be working from 7:00 a.m. until 3:00 p.m. The CPD finally figured out that it was burning out its police officers with this totally insane rotating schedule.

Thankfully, Chicago police officers are now assigned shifts on a yearly basis. Every November, officers bid for shift assignments for the following year by seniority. This shift-selection process has no effect on most specialized units, which are on different schedules that vary. These units can adjust their officers' tours of duty and even their regular days off, depending on their assignments and the types of crime problems they are assigned to handle.

One of the difficulties of transitioning from a brand-new rookie cop to a full-fledged police officer is that you aren't assigned a regular partner right away. Almost everyone is eventually paired with a permanent partner unless you're a dickhead who no one wants to work with. Partnerships can last months or even years, depending on how they get along. I've seen many partners who stayed together throughout their entire careers. I've also seen partners break up after only a few days together.

Once you leave your field-training officer, you're thrown into the general population, so to speak. The new guys are assigned to work as fill-ins—for example, if someone's partner is on vacation or off work due to an illness. During my first few months off probation, I was bounced around and assigned to work with many different officers. I don't remember all the cops I worked with during that time period, but some do stand out. I worked with an old-timer named Wally Gaywell.

Wally was a little over six feet tall and in average shape for a guy in his sixties; he wasn't heavy, but he wasn't skinny either. Wally was in the twilight of his police career. He kind of lumbered along at a slow pace, like he was in no hurry to get anywhere too quickly. After all, he had to kill an eight-hour day five days a week. Wally worked a foot post in the 12th District for many years, glad-handing with business owners and writing a few parking tickets each day. Not a real stressful job, as police work goes. The last thing Wally wanted to do was real police work at this stage in his career. The reason Wally got stuck working with me in a beat car was due to an argument over some stupid bullshit he had with a young and arrogant brand-new field lieutenant. The lieutenant got Wally dumped off his foot post that he had been assigned to for many years. He really wanted to stick it to Wally, so he was assigned to work with me as punishment. I was an aggressive and naive cop, known to be a loose cannon who drove like an out-of-control madman, which was exactly what Wally hated.

When hot in-progress calls came out over the police radio, I drove like a bat out of hell. I felt invincible; that mindset was reckless and stupid. At the time, it seemed so normal. In-progress calls were jobs assigned to a specific squad car in which the offender was still on the scene and the crime was in progress. Poor Wally was scared to death that I would kill him in a car accident on the way to a call. He went from working the slow pace of a foot post with very little action to working with me. A young and overly aggressive cop who took chances that bordered on stupidity. My driving really scared Wally more than anything, and he would always get into work early and grab our squad car keys. He told me that he liked driving, but I knew he just wanted to keep me from driving. Usually partners rotated driving, but I had to fight with Wally to share the driving duties.

Wally was innately a nervous person and when I drove he was always screaming at me to slow down. Wally also used to have a white ring around his mouth because he was always popping Rolaids antacids to counteract his burning stomach from the stress. It aggravated me to the point that I would speed up just to piss him off. I didn't become a cop to drive like an old lady. I loved the adrenalin rush of driving very fast through the city streets, lights flashing and siren blaring—the pure thrill of racing to wherever the real action took place. I was slowly becoming an adrenalin junkie; it was an addiction I would happily feed throughout my entire career. When I look back on it now, I now realize Wally was right, and I should have slowed down.

I was only involved in one major squad-car accident in my career, but I caused many of them due to the reckless way I drove my squad car when responding to hot in-progress calls. Wally taught me one of the most important lessons of my career. He always had his gun hanging down nearly to his knee. He also always had a pocket full of candy that he would pass out to people when we would go to calls. I wanted to get out and fight with people; Wally wanted to give them candy. I couldn't wait to get a more aggressive partner.

We were driving around on our beat one day when Wally said something to me that changed my entire career: "Pat, you can drive around forever, looking out this squad car window and learning very little. The only way you will ever know what's really happening on your beat is to get out and talk to people. Most people like to talk if you develop a rapport with them and make them feel comfortable with you. Just ask a lot of questions when you are talking to people and act interested in what they say. You'll be surprised at how much you can learn just by talking and listening to people on the street."

I drove poor Wally crazy, but not for too long; he eventually got back to his foot post and I moved on to other partners. Even though I didn't realize it at the time, Wally taught me one of the most valuable lessons I've learned on the job: to be an effective street cop and solve the crimes occurring on your beat, you needed information from the people on the street, and the only way to get that information was to talk to the people who lived and worked there. It really did change the course of my career. Wally made me realize how important street sources were if you wanted to be an effective street cop who made a lot of quality arrests.

As my career progressed through many different stages, the wisdom Wally shared with me when I was young and dumb, getting out and developing street sources and confidential informants (CIs), helped me more than I can say. It literally changed the course of my life, not just my career. In the later years of my police career, I would reflect back on the lessons I learned from Wally. I traveled throughout the United States and abroad on many complex and interesting cases because of the street sources and confidential informants I was able to develop. Wally set me on the right path and I benefited so much from the short time we worked together as partners. Thanks, Wally. Not many people had such a profound and positive effect on my career and my life as you did. It was an honor and a privilege to work with such a smart cop, and I wish that I had appreciated Wally as much back then as I do today.

≈≈≈≈≈

It makes me extremely sad to report that when I first came on the job, there was a small group of police officers who were straight-up thieves and bandits. Some of the cops were as bad as or even worse than the criminals we were trying to put in jail. These officers either wanted to work alone or with another cop who had the same mindset and was a thief. Early on in my career I got stuck working with rotten cops a few times, the ones who couldn't care less about doing real police work. They hit the street everyday with the intention of stealing as much money as they could during their tours of duty.

The Chicago Police Department had approximately 12,000 police officers, of which only a few were the proverbial bad apples. The corrupt officers were leery of the new officers, and they went to great lengths to feel you out to see if you would be interested in stealing along with them. The last thing a dishonest cop wanted was to work with an honest cop. I could tell almost immediately if the cop I was assigned to work with was a thief: he would get in the squad car and immediately talk about how low our pay was, how unfair it was for new officers who were just getting started out in life. The police department required us to live within the city limits of Chicago. On a cop's salary back then, it was almost impossible to buy a house in Chicago without financial help from your parents or a rich aunt or uncle.

The dishonest cops would always be complaining about the small amount of money we made as cops. Invariably, one would say to me, "Kid, they don't pay us shit for the hours we work and the risks we take." It was a clever tactic these corrupt cops used to feel you out. They wanted to know if you were the type of police officer who would be interested in making some extra cash to help your family get ahead. Some of these cops were nice guys on the surface, other than being thieves, so it was very uncomfortable to have these types of discussions with them.

I knew right away what was going on with these dishonest cops. I would tell the cop giving me the pitch, "That may be true, but I don't take traffic money or have any desire to do anything else dishonest, and I don't want to work with anyone who does. If you ever steal money in front of me and I'm questioned about it, I will probably give you up. I'm a nervous person and could never handle the pressure if IAD-internal affairs ever grabbed and questioned me. I'll give you up in a heartbeat."

It would almost be funny if it weren't so damn sad to see the looks of total disappointment on their faces; was really disturbing. After one of these discussions, I literally had one corrupt cop immediately drive me back to the district station and tell the watch commander that he didn't want to work with me. He told the watch commander on duty that we had a personality conflict and that we couldn't get along as partners. The only conflict we had was that he wanted to steal traffic money, and I wanted to do real police work.

The watch commander pulled me aside, called in another officer, and sheepishly said, "Pat, complete the rest of your shift with this officer. Some cops just don't get along. I wouldn't take it personal, kid." Today police corruption is handled entirely different. We still have a few bad cops who steal on the job, but they definitely are not as open about it as in earlier days.

In my twenty-six years with the department, I only witnessed a few instances of corruption firsthand. I remember once when I was in the locker room at the 12th District station, suiting up for my next tour of duty. I had been on the job for about a year and a half at the time. As I stood by my locker getting dressed for the street, I heard two police officers talking about a brand-new traffic signal that had been recently installed at the intersection of 18th and Halsted Streets in the south end of the district. There was already a traffic light at that intersection but they added a new turning arrow to help speed the flow of vehicle traffic. At first, when I heard these two officers talking about how great it was this new turning arrow had been installed, I was very impressed. I really thought I was hearing two cops talking about the new turning arrow that were honestly interested in traffic safety, but I couldn't have been more wrong.

As the two officers left the locker room, still all excited about the new turning arrow, I heard the one cop say to the other, "That turning arrow is going to be a real moneymaker!" What a reality check that was for me. A wave of disbelief and sadness hit me like a gut punch: These two assholes weren't interested in traffic safety at all. They just saw another way to make money by shaking down some poor citizen who committed a traffic violation in the district. I was really disturbed at the time how openly they talked about stealing traffic money.

As a young cop, I had another disturbing incident of theft on a job. I had been assigned to "a man shot" call on the fifth floor of a project building located at 1111 W. Roosevelt Road. I raced to the scene with my lights flashing and siren blaring. When I arrived, I climbed up the stairway to the fifth floor where I saw him lying there in a large pool of blood.

It was obvious to me that the shooting victim was definitely dead. He was lying on his back in the project stairway, a big chunk of his face and head had been blown away by what looked to have been a close-range shotgun blast. There was no real need to summon an ambulance; he was clearly dead. I radioed the dispatcher that we needed to notify the Homicide Division about the murder. Because I was the patrol car assigned to handle the shooting, it was my responsibility to fill out the initial case report on the incident; the homicide detectives from the Violent Crimes Unit would then handle the follow-up investigation and try to make an arrest. I made some preliminary notes about my observations at the crime scene and did an inventory list of the gunshot victim's personal property.

The murder victim's body was transported by a paddy wagon to Cook County Hospital to be pronounced. The paddy wagon, as they are known in police circles, is a truck-like vehicle used to transport prisoners and dead bodies. It's standard police procedure to transport any dead-on-arrival (DOA) to the nearest hospital to be officially pronounced dead by a certified medical doctor. Most of the time, the victim is left in the paddy wagon and a doctor from the emergency room comes out to make the official pronouncement of death. After being officially pronounced dead by a doctor, the body is then transported to the Cook County morgue for an autopsy. I canvassed the apartments near where the victim was shot to find out if anyone had heard or seen anything. I was unable to locate any witnesses who heard or saw anything suspicious, so after my canvass I headed to the morgue to complete my police report.

At the county morgue, I was met by an attendant who handed me a bag with the personal effects of the murder victim. When I checked the contents, I immediately noticed that the watch and ring the victim had on when I found him—and had noted on my initial report—were missing. I asked the morgue attendant about the missing watch and ring and he told me that the victim wasn't wearing either a watch or ring when he was brought into the morgue. I immediately realized that someone had taken these items from the victim's body.

I called my supervising sergeant and said, "Sarge, the watch and ring that I saw on my murder victim are now both missing."

The sergeant seemed very uncomfortable as he said, "Well, maybe you were mistaken and just *thought* you saw those items on the victim. That was a pretty gruesome scene, McCarthy. Maybe you didn't actually see them."

"No," I argued, "I *know* I saw the victim wearing them and they are in my report."

Much to my surprise, my sergeant then said, "Well, when you complete your final report, only include the items we currently possess."

It made me sick to my stomach to think that some asshole thief would steal some cheap costume jewelry, worth virtually nothing, from a murder victim in the projects. How fucking sad!

≈≈≈≈≈

The 12th District had a section called "skid row," a several-block stretch along Madison Street. It was a desperate place where down-on-their-luck alcoholics lived and usually died. So many bums lived in the flea-bag motels on and around skid row that the district actually had what they called the "bum wagon" to pick up these passed-out drunken derelicts and take them to an alcohol detoxification center so they wouldn't freeze to death out on the street. As a new cop in the district with no steady partner at the time, I was occasionally assigned to work the bum wagon with a veteran officer as a fill-in. The cops who worked the bum wagon were usually the old-timers in the district; they were often near retirement and had no desire to do any more real police work. These cops were just killing time until they retired to collect their pensions.

One day I experienced my first "stinker call." A stinker is a dead person who has usually died from complications from alcoholism and the body is not discovered for several days or even weeks. My partner and I received a DOA call at a flophouse apartment on South Halsted Street. It was your typical skid-row men's hotel, which is what they were called. The most severe alcoholics would rent rooms by the week, or sometimes even by the night, to sleep off their drunken stupors.

As we parked the bum wagon in front of the flophouse, the cop I was working with handed me a big cigar, saying, "You'll need this, kid."

"But I don't smoke cigars."

He just smiled at me as he lit his cigar.

The DOA we were assigned to handle was in a small men's hotel located on the second floor of a four-story building above a Greek restaurant. As soon as we opened the front door and started to walk up the narrow stairway to the second floor, the smell immediately hit me. The stench was just horrible, and now I knew why the old-timer offered me the cigar—the smoke from the cigar was to help mask the horrible smell of the decomposing body. We were directed to the tiny hotel room where the dead body was located. The manager directing us to the room was dirty and disheveled and looked like a bum himself. He acted as if it was no big deal that some poor down-on-his-luck alcoholic had died in his bed in his rented room. As we entered the hotel room, the dead guy was lying in bed on his back with his mouth and eyes wide open. Flies and maggots were crawling all over his face.

I had to brace myself against the wall as I tried to pull myself together. It was by far the creepiest sight that I had ever seen in my life. Little did I know at that time what the future had in store for me. I tried not to breathe the stench-filled air, but that was impossible. I felt nauseous and lightheaded as I stared at the dead guy's face in total and complete shock. The whole scene seemed surreal. I wanted to immediately run outside and breathe some fresh air. I wanted badly to wash away the frightening and repulsive sight I was looking at from my mind. I must have been as pale as a ghost and looked like I was about to pass out.

The old-time cop handed me the cigar and said, "Relax, kid, you'll be okay. Go outside, take a few deep breaths, and come back upstairs in a few minutes."

I couldn't wait to get the hell out of there. I literally ran down the stairs to get outside and away from this creepy room. As I stood in front of the building, trying to catch my breath, I was immediately struck by how normal everything else around me appeared to be. People were going about their daily business, walking up and down the street, oblivious to the gruesome scene only a short distance away. I was in total shock but still had to go back upstairs and deal with this poor dead alcoholic. This time I had a lit cigar in my mouth to help mask the terrible stench of death.

I would later learn another helpful trick from another old-timer to help me deal with stinkers in the future: "Pat, you take the filters off two cigarettes and stuff them up your nose. It only marginally diminishes the odor, but at least it's something to help cut down the horrible stench."

When I returned to the dead guy's room, my partner had already opened the windows to help air the place out, which helped slightly. We both smoked cigars as we wrapped the dead guy in his bed sheets and placed his body into a plastic body bag as blood, shit, and other bodily fluids oozed out of his rectum. We then drove the bum wagon to Cook County Hospital to have him officially pronounced dead before taking him to the county morgue.

I was lucky to have only had to work the bum wagon a few times in my career, but that was enough time for me to realize it wasn't for me. Dealing with dead bodies is a part of a being cop, but it was one aspect of the job I never got used to, even after twenty-six years on the job.

≈≈≈≈≈

One of the weirdest deaths I had to deal with in the 12th District occurred in the emergency room of Cook County Hospital, which is the real hospital used as the backdrop for the 1980s hit TV series "ER." One day I was assigned a DOA call in the emergency room of the hospital. Apparently, an obese lady, who weighed well over 400 lbs., came into the emergency room complaining of chest pain and shortness of breath. As she lay on the gurney in the emergency room waiting to be examined by a doctor, she suffered a massive heart attack and died suddenly. Efforts by emergency personnel to revive her failed, and she was pronounced dead.

We had to get her body from the hospital's emergency room to the Cook County morgue to determine the official cause of death. The dead woman was so heavy that it was impossible to lift her huge body off the hospital gurney for transference to the morgue. I called my supervising sergeant for some advice. My sergeant said, "We're going to have to get creative with this situation here." After a short pause he added, "Okay, the county morgue is only two blocks from the hospital, let's keep the dead woman on the gurney and wheel her body down the street to the morgue."

My partner, Pete Fisher remarked, "Can you believe we're actually doing this crazy shit?"

I just laughed because if I didn't laugh I'd probably be crying; this poor woman was once a real human being and I had to keep pushing the gurney. The woman was so overweight that her body almost looked like a young kid lying on top of a skateboard. We carefully tied her hands and feet together with pieces of rope, covered her body with a bed sheet, and wheeled it out of the hospital and down the handicap ramp out onto the street.

The supervising sergeant sent one squad car with flashing lights to lead the way to the morgue and another squad car took up the rear with its lights flashing. We were quite a sight, wheeling this poor woman's dead body down the street with a full police escort. As we made our way to the morgue, her body wobbled and shook several times. I thought she would either fall off the gurney or it would just collapse under her extreme weight. As we wheeled her body to the morgue, I kept thinking, *Just another day in the life of a cop.*

Most people have no real idea some of the crazy shit cops all over the country deal with on a daily basis.

≈≈≈≈≈

In mid-1977, after about a year in the district, I was finally assigned to work a regular beat car with two cops, Sam and Tom, and I was considered the "third man" on their regularly assigned patrol car. We were all assigned to a different "day-off group." The police department had a system by which every police officer was put into a day-off group numbered one though seven. For example, I was in day-off group seven, which meant that one week I would be off Monday and Tuesday; the next week I would be off Tuesday and Wednesday; the following week Wednesday and Thursday; and so on.

Every fifth week your weekend rotation came up, and you had three consecutive days off. The first weekend rotation, you'd be off Friday, Saturday, and Sunday; the next weekend it was Saturday, Sunday, and Monday. Sam, Tom, and I were in different day-off groups, meaning we rotated our days off; some days I was assigned to work with Sam, other days I was with Tom. When the time came that we all worked on an overlapping day, I would usually work with someone else on the watch whose regular partner was off that day. Both Sam and Tom were great guys, but they had completely different personalities and very different working styles.

Sam was a somewhat laid-back cop and not too aggressive on

the street. Tom was just the opposite: outgoing with a great sense of humor and a winning personality. Everyone in the district knew and liked him. On the street he was like an ambassador for the police department. Tom would grab every female's hand we encountered during our tours of duty and kiss it, no matter the situation. It didn't matter if the woman was eighty or ten years old, Tom was always kissing their hands; he was a major-league charmer.

Tom constantly talked to everybody on our beat, making a real effort to get to know everybody personally; he was always upbeat, happy-go-lucky, and full of energy. Sam, on the other hand, was quiet and more reserved. He wasn't really that into being a street cop and only did the minimum work required to get by. In my entire twenty-six-year career as a cop, I never saw anyone work harder to get out of work than Sam.

The beat we patrolled had three different hospitals: the University of Illinois Hospital, Presbyterian-Saint Luke's Hospital, and Cook County Hospital. All were located within a few short blocks from each other on our beat. People from all over the city made their way to these hospitals for treatment of various illnesses and injuries. We had gunshot victims who either drove themselves or had someone take them to one of these hospitals after being shot in different areas of the city. Because these three hospitals were located on our beat, we were responsible for writing the police reports on the people transported there after being shot in other parts of the city. One of the things that surprised me the most, as I learned the ropes of being a big-city cop, was that every year thousands of people are shot and stabbed in Chicago.

Cook County Hospital was the most common place they would wind up after being shot, because it had a trauma center that specialized in treating gunshot victims. Everyone in the ghetto knew that if you were shot or stabbed you went to the county hospital for the best treatment. It was also well known throughout the police department that if a cop got shot, Cook County Hospital's trauma center was the best place to take them.

We often received radio assignments to handle gunshot victims at the county hospital; most weren't serious. We dealt with many graze wounds and gunshot wounds in which the bullets would pass through the victims' bodies without hitting anything vital like a bone or body organ. If I was working with Tom and we got a "gunshot victim" call, we went to the hospital and completed a police report for an "aggravated battery incident." A police report contains general information about how the person was shot, when the shooting occurred, and the incident location. It is a brief, one-page police report that takes only about ten or fifteen minutes to prepare. The report is then forwarded to the proper police district and detective division area where the shooting had occurred for a follow-up investigation to be conducted.

If I was working with Sam and we got this type of "gunshot victim" call, it was an entirely different situation. At the hospital, Sam would talk to the victim in a very warm and sincere tone of voice, almost like a whisper as if he was a parish priest consoling a distraught parishioner who had just experienced a traumatic incident in their lives.

He put his hand on the shoulder of the gunshot victim and in the most sincere voice said," I know you're scared and very upset right now. You just experienced something no one should have to ever experience. After traumatic events like this, people are usually not thinking clearly. It's going to take some time for you to get your thoughts together to figure out exactly what happened. Go home, relax a little bit, and talk over what happened with your family. You can call the local district police later when you're in better shape to file a police report."

All Sam was trying to do was get out of making an "aggravated battery incident" police report, which would only have taken us ten to fifteen minutes to fill out. When Sam was successful, we just filled out a little, three-by-six inch orange card called a "miscellaneous incident report." The "miscel-X card," as it was known as in the police department, had the basic information with a short narrative section. This is where Sam would say that the victim was not interested in filing an official police report at that time. Sam would put the card in the breast pocket of his uniform shirt and walk out of the hospital, proud of himself that he avoided writing a police report. It was just plain stupid and nothing more than a lazy cop who didn't want to do his job properly.

Chapter 6

To Serve and Protect

One of the hardest adjustments I had to make when working in the housing projects was that the police who worked there were viewed by most residents as the enemy. I really wanted to help the people in my district; I wanted to make them feel safer and solve some of the out-of-control gang and drug problems they had to deal with daily. Police are there to serve and protect, which is difficult to accomplish when the people you are supposed to be serving and protecting don't even want you there. The living conditions in most of the project buildings were deplorable. Many of the people living in them were good, honest, hard-working people who deserved better—but they didn't have a chance to live a normal life. The gang bangers and drug dealers ran the show; they literally controlled the project buildings.

I often heard veteran cops say that being a cop was a thankless job. In many situations you're "damned if you do and damned if you don't." In Chicago we have a system known as "parity," which means whatever raise the police or firefighters get, the other department receives the same raise. However, firefighters only work about ninety days a year. I often heard the bullshit argument: "When it's 10° below zero and we're pulling hose, we earn our money." That's bullshit to the police, though, because we are there directing traffic around all your hoses when it's 10° below zero, too. Don't get me wrong; I love firefighters. I have two sisters who were with the Chicago Fire Department. My sister Maureen still works there, and my sister Judy recently retired after twenty years. I have a saying about firefighters: They sleep until they get hungry, and then eat until they get tired again! But I'll get back to the real issue at hand.

When the police leaned on area criminals with street stops and pat-down searches to stem the flow of guns and drugs in and around the projects, we were viewed as an occupying force, the evil white-racist enemy. Even black police officers were viewed as the enemy by the projects' residents; they were commonly referred to as "Uncle Tom" sellouts, who were just tools for the white man. It's even worse for police officers today; honest, hard-working cops get so little respect.

I know damned well that, unfortunately, there are some prejudiced or unbalanced cops out there who view all citizens, no matter their ethnic backgrounds, as the enemy. However, from what I've seen, they are the small minority—*but,* they get the most press. Over 99% of police officers put their lives on the line every day, trying to stem the violence and criminal activity in big cities and small towns all across this country. It has always frustrated me that, even as I worked hard and tried to help people living in the projects, there was so much mistrust and outright hatred toward anyone who wore a uniform or carried a badge and a gun.

If the police took a day off and let the public know in advance that no police action would be taken for the next twenty-four hours, it would be anarchy. People would figure out real fast how fucked up the country would be without the police out there risking everything to protect them.

I also know that most cops perform heroic things on a daily basis with little or no thanks or recognition for their dangerous work; it's just part of the job. Every day, situations in the ghetto that would horrify average citizens are handled with professionalism and a great deal of pride by the dedicated police officers working there. These officers risk their very lives to help the people who need police protection the most.

The things you see, feel, and experience almost daily as an officer can only be truly understood by other cops having these same experiences. It would be like describing Marine Corps boot camp to someone who has never experienced it. You might get a feel for what it's like by watching a movie or hearing someone talking about it, but the old saying applies, "Until you've walked a mile in my shoes . . . ." I've experienced things as a cop that, even to this day, I have a hard time believing and am glad most people don't have to experience.

I once walked backward down nine flights of stairs with a woman who had just slit both her wrists with a razor blade in a suicide attempt. The elevators were out of order at the time, which was a common occurrence in the project buildings. My partner and I called for an ambulance to transport the woman to the hospital and were told that no ambulances were available. We would have to transport the victim by a paddy wagon or squad car to the hospital. We wrapped the injured woman's badly cut wrists with wet T-shirts to help stem the flow of blood. My partner and I pushed and pulled her down the stairway.

All the way down the nine flights of stairs, I tightly held her wrists as she cried and tried to pull away, snot and tears running down her face while she kept saying, "I just want to die!"

Over and over I kept telling her, "Everything will be okay. Everything will be okay."

My partner and I finally got her into our squad car and transported her to the hospital. As my partner drove the squad car, lights flashing and siren blaring, I sat in the backseat holding this poor woman's wrists very tightly so she wouldn't bleed to death on the way to the hospital. I kept telling my partner, "Step on it! We really need to get to the hospital fast." Luckily, her suicide attempt failed and we did save her life.

It really bothered me that no matter how hard we tried or how many great things we did for the people in the projects, we were still viewed as the enemy. It may sound corny, but it was true: I really did want to help and have a positive impact on those peoples' lives, even if it was just in a small way.

≈≈≈≈≈

Having no ambulances available in the 12th District—even with three hospitals—was a lot more common than most people would think, especially on busy, hot summer nights. I was working the 4:00 p.m. to midnight shift one hot Friday night and received a "two men shot" radio call. A gang fight had broken out between two rival street gangs, the 26ers and the Latin Counts, at a street carnival in the predominantly Hispanic section of the district that night. One gang member pulled out a gun during the fight and fired several shots, wounding two people. I was the first patrol car to respond to the scene of the shooting.

When I arrived, the street was blocked off by city barricades to keep traffic out of the carnival area. The streets were crowded with hundreds of people who were having a good time, partying and drinking beer, when these idiot gang bangers decided to act stupidly toward each other, which resulted in a violent gang fight and a double shooting.

A pretty young teenage girl came running up to my squad car, frantically crying, "My brother and his friend have just been shot there," as she pointed down the street.

I asked, "Where are they now, and who shot them?" but she didn't answer.

She was in shock and just kept yelling, "Please help them! Please help them!" as she ran off down the street back to where her brother and his friend lay wounded on the ground.

Other people approached me and told me that the shooting had taken place just down the block, pointing in the direction where the young girl had just run off. I parked my squad car and ran toward the shooting scene. I immediately radioed the dispatcher: "Two people have been shot, and I need two ambulances to transport both victims to the hospital. Now! The victims are located in the 1700 block of 18th Street."

Most people at the street carnival were laughing and having a good time, unaware of the shooting; Mexican salsa music was blaring loudly from all directions as I made my way through the crowd. A large group of people had gathered in a circle around the two street-gang members lying on the ground. As I broke through the circle, the two shooting victims were being assisted by people from the large crowd now around them.

I immediately radioed the dispatcher: "Two people have been shot and I need two ambulances to transport both victims to the hospital—now."

I was told, "No ambulances are available at this time. I will have to send two paddy wagons as transport."

As I surveyed the scene, I saw that one of the victims was in very bad shape. He was unconscious, lying face up in a large pool of blood with the pale-gray look of someone who is about to die. It was a look I had seen many times before in my short career as a cop. The other victim was still conscious and crawling around on all fours, trying to get up. People from the crowd tried to get him to lie down, but he was in a state of shock.

Frustrated, I got back on the radio: "Hey, this is serious! One victim is in very bad shape and might not make it. We need at least one ambulance immediately!"

The dispatcher only said, "I'll see what I can do," and rang off.

This isn't good enough, I angrily thought. Other officers began to arrive on the scene to assist me.

Trying to comfort the gang banger who was still conscious, I said, "Hang on, help is on the way. I know you'll be okay. Just stay awake! What's your name? Can you tell me who shot you, so we can find him and make sure he pays for this?"

He looked me in the eye and could barely get out, "My name is Jose. Am I going to die, officer?"

"No, I'm sure you'll be fine; we just need to get you to the hospital."

"I don't know who shot me or why!" the kid pleaded, which I

knew was pure bullshit.

A paddy wagon finally arrived and loaded up the more seriously wounded victim and sped off to the hospital, leaving the other victim still on the ground. The young girl who originally approached me was now completely hysterical. As the other officers and I waited for another paddy wagon to arrive, she was screaming right in my face, "Do something! Why can't you do something?"

Then the crowd started chanting, "Do something! Do something!" over and over again.

Even though it was only minutes, it seemed like forever since the first paddy wagon had left to transport the other victim.

I radioed dispatch again: "Listen! Things are starting to get out of hand here! The crowd is pissed, and we really needed another paddy wagon right away to transport the second victim."

"I'm sorry but it's a busy night, and the only thing I can do is request a wagon from a neighboring district. And I'm not sure how long it will take to get to you."

I don't know what people think police officers on the ground can do in situations like this with no backup, but we had to do something before a riot started. The chants of "Do something" were getting louder and angrier, so we wound up putting the second gunshot victim in the backseat of a squad car just to get him off the street before the second paddy wagon finally arrived. Then we got the hell out of there before a riot broke out.

≈≈≈≈≈

Most of the radio calls police officers are required to handle on a regular basis are usually a lot less serious than the one I just described. The most common call for most police departments around the country is for "domestic disturbance." It can also potentially be one of the deadliest calls; every year, many police officers are killed or seriously injured while handling "domestic disturbance" calls. I was involved in many of these types of calls in my first few years on the job, but one stands out in my mind as special.

My partner Tommy Weaver and I handled a "domestic disturbance" call once where a woman's boyfriend was drunk and slapping her around. When we responded to the call, her asshole boyfriend had already left the apartment. A cute little African-American boy, about nine or ten years old, met us at the apartment door. The poor kid was crying his eyes out. We entered the apartment and found the mother and several other small kids inside; everybody was crying. We later learned this woman had several kids by different fathers.

My partner and I tried to diffuse the situation: "Let's try to remain calm here. Everything will be okay. Just tell us what happened."

The mother said, "My boyfriend and I got into a fight over some stupid bullshit, and he started slapping me around. When my son tried to protect me, my boyfriend slapped him around pretty good too. He's drunk and not the kid's father. I just don't know what to do anymore!"

We filed a report as my partner Tommy and I worked hard to try to comfort the kids, who were extremely upset and crying uncontrollably. I said, "Don't worry, we'll find this guy and lock him up in jail. He won't be able to hurt any of you again. But if he does show back up here before we can catch him, dial 911, and we'll be back in an instant to take him to jail."

Even though I was sure these children had seen this kind of shit before, it was still tough on them. No kid should have to live like that. I've seen some of the toughest cops fall apart emotionally when a violent incident involving young kids occurred. There's something about seeing a small child hurt or crying that triggers deep-seated, protective emotions. I'll admit, I was one of the worst when it came to seeing little kids abused and suffering; it really tore me up. I learned to compartmentalize it in my mind and handled some pretty outrageous shit in my twenty-six-year career as a cop, but to this day, some of the terrible things I witnessed happening to young kids still bother me.

As I continued to try to comfort the young kid who was slapped around during this domestic disturbance, I felt totally helpless. He was sobbing and really scared. Unfortunately, I also knew this wouldn't be the last time the poor kid would see the police in his apartment.

I didn't know what else to do, so I pulled out a five-dollar bill from my pocket and said, "Here you go; buy something fun with this."

His mood immediately changed and his tears started to quickly dry up as he said, "Gosh, thank you so much!"

I said, "I know it doesn't seem like it now, but everything will be okay, and we'll get him." It was amazing how many times I would use the sentence, "Everything will be okay" in my career, even though I often knew it was pure bullshit when I said it. In the ghetto, things were rarely "okay," regardless of how hard we tried to help the residents. Sometimes it was the only thing I could think of to say to comfort people at the time.

I asked the kid, "What school do you go to?" When he told me the school, I added, "What do you want to be when you grow up?"

Much to my surprise, he said, "I want to be a cop just like you. Do you know where I could get a job after school to make some money?"

I answered, "Buddy, I'll keep my eyes open and if I hear of anything, I'll let you know." I left the apartment with a very heavy heart. I felt so sorry for those little kids and the conditions they were forced to live in I wanted to cry myself. The real-life world of the ghetto can be a pretty fucked-up place for some people to live. My partner was as upset as I was and we both wanted to tune-up this guy: in plain English, give him a few cracks he definitely deserved. Tommy and I cruised the neighborhood, looking for the boyfriend for a short period of time, until we were given another job to handle. That guy was lucky we didn't spot him that night on the street; we were in no mood to be our usual friendly selves if we had found him.

I told Tom, "I'm sure that asshole was drunk enough to have put up some resistance if we grabbed him and tried to handcuff him for the beatings in the apartment."

Tom agreed and said, "What kind of rotten prick would slap around a young kid like that?"

I asked him, "What do you think the odds are that the asshole will show back up at the apartment tonight?"

"I really doubt he will, Pat. He knows we were there and he knows he'd probably get locked up if he showed back up there tonight."

Several days later, while I was on routine street patrol, I stopped at a grocery store on my beat for a short break. As I stood at the counter to pay for my soda, I felt a tug on my shirtsleeve. I looked down and saw standing next to me the young boy who had been slapped around by his mother's boyfriend during the domestic disturbance I just described.

He asked me in a cute little voice, "Hey, did you find me a job yet?"

I was a little surprised to see him in the store, but I recognized him immediately, and said, "Hi there, good to see you. I'm still looking for a job for you but haven't found the right one yet." I reached into my pocket and handed him a couple bucks to buy some candy. I asked him, "Have you seen you mom's boyfriend since that night?"

He replied, "No, my momma's got a new boyfriend now. We ain't seen that old one since you came to our apartment."

After a few minutes of small talk, I said my goodbyes and left the store with tears welling up in my eyes. I thought, How sad that this young, innocent kid doesn't have a chance in hell to lead a normal life. He's got to go back to that ghetto apartment and be a bit player in his mother's fucked-up lifestyle.

Life just isn't fair sometimes, especially when you grow up in the ghetto.

Chapter 7

Losing My Hero

As time passed, I slowly started to feel more comfortable in my role as a cop. I couldn't know it at the time, but I was headed toward the saddest day of my life and I never saw it coming. My dad had severe diabetes and was in the hospital for some routine tests because he hadn't been feeling well. I got a call from my mother at 5:00 a.m. in June of 1977. She was crying and told me that St. Anne's Hospital had just called and said that my dad had experienced some complications overnight and she needed to get to the hospital right away. I was in total shock. I had just visited him in the hospital the night before, and he seemed perfectly fine. Being a cop, I knew that the hospital doesn't notify a patient's family at 5:00 a.m. unless it is something serious.

My mom, two brothers, four sisters, and I quickly raced to the hospital. One bad thing about being a cop is that you learn to read other people simply from being on the job. I saw the look on the nurse's face as soon as I walked into the hospital and immediately knew the situation was critical. We were ushered into a small room just down the hall from my dad's room. My entire family was told the bad news by a very somber doctor: my dad had suffered a massive stroke during the night. The night nurse had done a routine check on my dad and found him unconscious and unresponsive. The hospital preformed an emergency CT scan on him and found no brain activity. The doctor explained that the stroke was severe, and my dad was technically brain-dead.

My dad passed away several days later, after clinging to life on a respirator. He was only fifty years old. The day he passed away, June 23, 1977, was sadly also the seventeenth birthday of the twins Jim and Jean, the youngest in my family. My entire family spent those final days of my dad's life holding his hands and telling him how much we loved him. My dad was really a hero to everyone in my family. He wasn't perfect, but he was one hell of a man. For many years, my dad had a gambling and drinking problem. My mom finally had had enough, and no one blamed her for filing for a divorce. My parent's divorce was finalized on November 22, 1963, which happened to be the same day President John F. Kennedy was assassinated by sniper Lee Harvey Oswald in Dallas, Texas.

My dad was a great guy with a super-friendly personality; every one of my buddies loved and respected him. The city park where we hung out as kids was located about a block from my house; Wells Park was our home away from home. My dad would drive his unmarked squad car right over the curb and onto the grass, right up to where my buddies and I would be playing baseball.

We were all fascinated by the squawking sound of the Chicago police radio coming from inside his squad car. To us, it sounded like something you would see on some TV cop show. As I listened intently to the police radio, I had a hard time making out what the dispatcher was saying; it all seemed so garbled. I remember one time my dad had pulled up in the park with his squad car to see us and, as we talked, he suddenly got a call of a "burglary in progress." My dad jumped back into his squad car and roared off, spinning his tires, and kicking up grass and dirt, siren blaring as he sped off toward the call. My friends were so impressed, and I was bursting with pride. I knew that someday, I, too, would also lead an exciting life of action and adventure as a Chicago cop, just like my dad.

Another one of my fondest memories of my father—and I have many—was when my dad became the barber for many of the neighborhood kids, almost by accident. To save money, my dad would give my two brothers, Mike and Jimbo, and me haircuts in the backyard of our house. The barber "kit" my dad used was just a cheap buzz saw of an electric haircutter. Depending on the length of the cut, you could put a plastic attachment on the razor end that would cut the hair to the exact length you wanted it. But my dad never used the attachments; he just buzzed the shit out of our heads, right down to almost bare skin, exposing bumps, weird dents, and scars. At first, my brothers and I were horrified at our bald heads when we looked into the mirror. My dad was pretty slick, though, and told us that these were special haircuts; he called them "detective haircuts." It's amazing how bullshit sells.

Pretty soon, everyone in the neighborhood wanted a detective haircut. My dad would bring one of our kitchen chairs out to the backyard, get a long extension cord, and set up his portable barbershop. He would buzz through many of the neighborhood kids heads, giving them all detective haircuts; due to my dad, almost every kid in my neighborhood sported a detective haircut.

My father was also well-known throughout the Chicago Police Department. His wake and funeral were attended by a large contingent of police officers, detectives, and command staff from the department, including his boss and close friend, Commander Michael O'Donnell. My father and O'Donnell grew up as kids together in an Irish neighborhood on the west side of Chicago. They were both members of the 4400 Club, a group of Irish guys who'd grown up in that neighborhood. Many of my dad's friends became Chicago cops, with several rising up through the ranks to top command positions in the department.

Mike O'Donnell had also been the best man at my parents' wedding. At my dad's wake, Commander O'Donnell pulled me off to the side, gave me his business card, and said, "Pat, your dad was a great man. I had some of the best times of my life hanging out with your dad when we were growing up. If you ever need anything or I can help you out on the job, give me a call. I hope you know how proud of you your father was. Now keep an eye on your mother."

I said, "Thank you for saying such great things about Dad. It really means the world to me to hear that my dad was proud of me." I broke down crying as he gave me a big hug and several pats on the back.

He then slowly walked away with tears in his eyes, and said, "Hang in there, Pat."

Losing my father was a devastating blow to my entire family. We all worshipped him. Even though my dad had had problems for many years, he straightened his life out and attended Alcoholics Anonymous. He was even assigned to a special CPD unit for about a year that helped police officers with drinking problems. As I had mentioned earlier, my parents were divorced on the day President John F. Kennedy was killed in 1963. They eventually remarried seven years later on the anniversary date of their original wedding.

≈≈≈≈≈

Several months after we buried my dad, I went to see Mike O'Donnell at his office in the old 7th District – Maxwell Street police station on the near-south side of Chicago. I was taking Commander O'Donnell up on his offer to help me out on the job because I wanted a new assignment. In order to get assigned to a specialized unit in the Chicago Police Department, you had to have a sponsor—or as it was commonly referred to on the job, a "Chinaman." The term Chinaman is just slang for a powerful contact in either the world of politics or a big boss on the police department. In the city of New York, the term "Rabbi" is used, which means the same thing as Chinaman does in Chicago. Clout not only works on the police department and fire department, but also for any City of Chicago job.

You could be the hardest-working, best cop on the force, but without a phone call from someone with some political clout within the city or the police department, you had a slim chance of getting accepted into specialized units, such as the Gangs Crimes Unit or the Narcotics Section. That's just how things were done in the city back then. In reality, I don't think much has changed since then. It might not be quite as out in the open as it used to be, but anyone who knows how Chicago works knows what I'm talking about.

A famous saying in Chicago, which I think was attributed to the late Mayor Richard J. Daley, was: "We don't want nobody; nobody sent." In other words, someone with some clout had to sponsor you (i.e., make a call for you) if you ever expected to get into a specialized unit. Even though O'Donnell and my father were lifelong friends and he was the best man at my parent's wedding, I had only seen him a few times in my life. I hardly knew him, and I was quite nervous about asking him for a favor. Commander O'Donnell was in charge of the Vice Control Division, which included the Gambling, Prostitution, and Intelligence Unit and the Narcotics Unit. The unit I wanted very badly to get into was narcotics. It was a down-and-dirty assignment that dealt with the evil people who were selling and using dope. Ever since that day in the Police Academy when the young Hispanic narcotics cop gave that talk to my recruit class about the narcotics unit and how they operated on the street, I was hooked and desperately wanted the thrill and adrenaline rush of narcotics work.

As I parked my car in front of the Maxwell Street police station, thoughts of my dad rushed through my head. I sat in my car and had a short talk with my dad. Some people might think I'm crazy to "talk" to my dad, but still, to this day, it helps me to share my thoughts with him. My dad is buried in St. Joseph's Cemetery, which is located at Belmont and Cumberland in the small suburb of River Grove, Illinois. I thought of all the times my dad had parked in front of this very building and reported into work as a vice cop. As I walked into the police station, up the very same stairs my dad had walked thousands of times over the years, I felt a strong closeness with my dad, which was warm and comforting, but also sad at the same time.

I anxiously approached the front desk of the Maxwell Street station with sweaty palms and a nervous stomach. As I entered his office, Commander O'Donnell walked out from behind his desk with a big smile and a hearty handshake to greet me.

The first thing he said to me was, "I can't believe how much you remind me of your dad." After we shook hands, he told me to sit down, pointing to one of the two chairs that were directly in front of his desk. He couldn't have been any friendlier toward me, which made my nervousness start to slowly fade away.

He went out of his way to once again say, "Your father was the best and I feel lucky that we were friends for most of our lives. He made growing up in the west side of Chicago so much fun. Say, how's your mom and the rest of the family doing?"

I was happy to report, "Everyone is doing fine."

"Pat, I've heard some really good things about you and your work here. Your dad would be very proud of you."

"Thanks again for the kind words, Commander. It means the world to me and I miss my dad every day." I then anxiously said, "The reason I wanted to see you is that I want to get into the department's Narcotics Unit, and I hope you can put in a good word for me. While I really love being a uniformed beat cop, I've always dreamed of working in plain clothes as an undercover cop in the Narcotics Unit. I want more action than we get working in uniformed patrol."

He laughed and smiled at me as I nervously rambled on about my desire to get into Narcotics work. When I finally shut up, he slowly leaned back in his chair as if he was in deep thought for a minute. He then leaned forward in a serious manner and said, "Pat, narcotics work is a dirty business. I've seen many young police officers, even those with the best of intentions, get jammed up and ruin careers—even their lives. The amount of temptation in the Narcotics Unit is far greater than in any other aspect of police work."

Shaking his head from side to side, he continued, "The broads, the booze, and the bucks are very often too much for many young cops to handle. I really don't feel comfortable sending you to narcotics, Pat." I was immediately crushed by his response and sat there in stunned silence. Then Commander O'Donnell asked, "Would you consider going into the Special Operations Unit, though, Pat?"

As an alternative to narcotics work, he explained that Special Operations was a citywide unit that concentrated mainly on felony cases and making gun arrests, adding, "You'll get plenty of 'real police action' in Special Operations; this unit often works in various and unique plainclothes assignments."

There was nothing I could say to Commander O'Donnell but, "Yes, of course I'd love to go to Special Operations, boss." Commander O'Donnell and I talked for a little while about my dad and some of the crazy shit O'Donnell and my dad did when they were young kids growing up on the west side of Chicago. As I sat in O'Donnell's office, hearing him tell me stories about my dad as a kid, I realized the old saying was true: "The apple doesn't fall far from the tree." I was a lot more like my dad than I had previously realized. I not only had some of my dad's facial features, I also inherited some of his wild side. I thanked O'Donnell for seeing me and told him that I would work very hard in Special Operations and that I would never embarrass him.

The Special Operations Unit worked the entire city. The unit handled any mass demonstrations and disturbances. It also worked special operations on the city's transit systems: both the CTA buses and El trains, looking for pickpocket suspects and other thieves and robbers. Much of this was undercover work, and it was a good place for me to start. The unit was also a highly mobile force that could be deployed at a moment's notice to any unusual criminal activity.

The unit was well known for not taking any shit from anybody. The Special Operations Unit used to be called the Task Force until some higher-ups, who had no idea that almost every year in the United States approximately 15,000 people are murdered, thought that the name sounded too intimidating. So in the mid-1970s, the name was changed to Special Operations Unit.

There was a saying in the unit: "One Riot, One Ranger," meaning that whenever any bad shit was going down in the city—whether it was an El train crash with multiple injuries, a plane crash, or just your average riot where stupid people decided to burn down and loot their neighborhoods—we were called. We also handled Nazi demonstrations and marches through mostly black neighborhoods, which often turned violent. It was the job of Special Ops coppers to handle the problems.

Now the new trend is called "flash mobs," where people are notified through social media to go to a certain location, such as the lakefront or Michigan Avenue, to beat up and rob anyone they can. It's sad that in an international city like Chicago, these often very violent incidents are kept pretty quiet; seldom do they get more than a down-played version in the newspapers or on TV newscasts. I think people should be aware of the real shit that goes on in the city.

After my meeting with Commander O'Donnell and his promise that I would be transferred into Special Operations, I had to put in a personal action request (PAR) form for transfer into the Special Operations Unit. After the form is completed, it is submitted to your district or unit secretary. The district secretaries were all patrol officers who handled the everyday administrative duties of the police district inside the station. They didn't deal directly with the public like the regular desk officers did. The district secretaries worked in a back office, taking care of attendance reports like tracking medical leave, injured on-duty reports, and vacation administrative paperwork.

When I submitted my PAR form for a transfer to Special Operations to the 12th District secretary, who was a seasoned veteran, he looked it over and asked me point-blank, "Okay, McCarthy, so who's your clout?"

I lied, "I don't have any clout."

He just laughed and said, "Right. I'm just going to put your request right into the circular filing cabinet because that's where it's going to wind up anyway with no clout." The circular file cabinet was the garbage can next to his desk. I just smiled at him and left the secretary's office, feeling pretty damn good about my future with Special Operations.

An unwritten rule on the Chicago Police Department is that you never give up your "Chinaman"—your clout—to anyone for fear that it might cause a problem for the Chinaman trying to help you out; in my case that was Commander O'Donnell. No matter how "heavy" you think your Chinaman/clout is, there are probably other Chinamen out there with more clout than yours. It's a weird power game that has been played out in Chicago for years.

I spent the next month working uniformed patrol in a beat car in the 12th District. It was great to know that I would soon be transferred into the elite Special Operations Unit.

Chapter 8

SPECIAL OPERATIONS

The Special Operations Unit was divided into three sections that were spread throughout the entire city: south, west, and north. I was going to Special Operations North, located at Belmont and Western Avenue. Special Operations North was responsible for policing nine north-side police districts, which had 350 to 400 police officers assigned to each district. Special Operations North covered the entire north side of the city and a small portion of the near-south side, but, as I mentioned earlier, we could be deployed to any area of the city at a moment's notice. It was a unit that took great pride in having some of the brightest and most aggressive police officers in the CPD.

It didn't matter to me what the unit was called; my new assignment in Special Operations was going to give me the constant, nonstop action I became a cop to experience. The Special Operations North office was located only about a mile from my childhood home on Leavitt Street, so the area was quite familiar to me. As I drove up to the building for the first time, I was struck by how much newer and bigger it was than the tiny 12th District – Monroe station. It even had a large parking lot so officers didn't have to park their personal vehicles and squad cars on the street or sidewalks, like they did in the 12th District. It was a large facility; back then, it was called the Area 6 building, and it housed the 19th District – Town Hall, the Area 6 Detective and Youth Divisions, and the Special Operations North Unit.

Back in the day, and up until just a few years ago, the police department had six detective divisions spread throughout the city. They were all located on the second floors of newer and larger police district buildings. The detective units were called "Areas" and numbered 1 through 6. So uniform patrol officers, who patrolled in marked squad cars, worked out of the ground floor of the building, and the plainclothes detectives were housed on the second floor. This floor had desks for the detectives and interview-and-interrogation rooms for questioning witnesses and interrogating suspects.

The Special Operations North office was located on the first floor at the far northeast corner of the building. It was a small section of the building that was subdivided into four connecting small offices: the captain's office with a desk area and a personal bathroom, the sergeant's office, the secretary's office, and the general-duty office.

I entered Area 6 and was directed down the hall to my new assignment by the 19th District desk sergeant on duty. I noticed the sign hanging on the wall just outside the office that said *Special Operations Unit*, which to me it was a beautiful sight. I was excited as hell to finally get a chance to do hardcore police work on a daily basis.

I nervously approached the desk officer, who was seated just inside the entrance door and said, "My name is Pat McCarthy, and I'm reporting for duty—just transferred in from the 12th District."

He gave me a funny look and said, "The captain wants to see you right away." He pointed to another connecting office door just to his left.

I knocked on the partially opened office door with a plaque that read: *Captain's Office.* A gruff voice instructed, "Well, come in."

The captain was a rough-looking, old-school Irish guy named Jack Walsh. I could immediately tell by the stern look on his face that he wasn't too happy to see me in his office.

"I'm Officer Pat McCarthy, Sir. I just transferred in from the 12th District and am officially reporting for duty."

The captain didn't shake my hand or make any other welcoming gesture toward me other than to say, "Sit down," as he pointed to one of two chairs that stood in front of his desk. He got right down to business and said, "Who's your clout, McCarthy?"

I played stupid and said, "Sir, I don't know what you mean."

He then appeared agitated as he asked, "I mean who helped you to get transferred into Special Operations?"

I lied to protect Commander O'Donnell: "Boss, I didn't talk to anyone about my transfer; I just submitted a PAR form, requesting a transfer into the unit."

The captain looked at me like I had just asked him for sex; his face turned bright red and his intense stare told me he was obviously pissed off. He said, "Listen kid, I wasn't born yesterday. Who the fuck do you know?"

I again played dumb. "I don't know anyone, Sir."

The captain then started yelling, "I know you're full of shit, *and* I know you're lying. I didn't request you, and I don't want you in this unit." He then added, " I'll be keeping a close eye on you, McCarthy, and if you fuck up in any way, you'll be gone in a heartbeat. I don't care who your clout is." He then angrily motioned for me to get out of his office by pointing to the door.

I was in total shock, having expected a somewhat warmer welcome. I left the captain's office, probably as pale as a ghost. The desk guy I had talked to when I first walked into the office must have heard how Captain Walsh greeted me because when I left the captain's office, he shot me a weird look and said, "Roll call is being held in the basement of the station—just past the radio room on the right hand side of the hallway. Come back and see me after roll call and I'll give you a locker assignment."

All cops are assigned a locker, which was usually located in the basement of the district station or area they worked in. The locker was where cops kept their uniforms, shoes or boots, and other equipment, such as shoe polish and a clean towel to dry off if they took a shower in one of the few shower stalls located in the locker room.

I walked downstairs to my first roll call in Special Operations, still somewhat shocked by what had just taken place in Captain Walsh's office. I thought to myself, *Man, Captain Walsh is a real asshole. I'm here to work for him.*

I knew I had a good reputation in the 12th District as a hardworking beat cop and that I was well suited to be a Special Ops cop. As it turned out, I proved myself as a hard worker over time, making many quality arrests, and I eventually became one of Captain Walsh's "go-to guys," a cop he could count on to give any assignment a 100% effort.

I found the roll-call room, which also had a sign that read *Special Operations* on the wall next to the door. Even after having my ass chewed out in the captain's office, I loved seeing that sign; it gave me a tremendous rush of pride.

I will never forget my first Special Operations roll call. It was like walking into a scene right out of the John Belushi movie *Animal House*, which was about a college fraternity house that was totally out of control. There were about twenty cops scattered around a room the size of an average public school classroom. Some were sitting in chairs; others were standing around the room talking to each other. Guys were yelling and throwing wadded-up daily bulletins at each other. It seemed as if they were all talking at the same time.

I entered the roll-call room and grabbed the closest chair I could find near the back of the room; no one even noticed me. This roll call was quite a contrast to my first roll call in the 12th District. I quickly noted that every cop in the room had at least two guns on them; most officers wore shoulder holsters with 9mm semiautomatics or .45 calibers and .38 caliber revolvers on their sides.

The first person to approach me stuck his hand out and said, "Hi, I'm Mike Byrne. Welcome to Special Ops. What district are you coming from?"

As we talked, Mike's partner walked up and said, "Hi, I'm Lenny Ciangi." As I talked to Ciangi and Burn, an older cop with silver-grey hair sat down in the seat right next to me.

He reached over and grabbed my right hand, saying, "You're a nice looking kid. Are you married?" I immediately pulled my hand away as he smiled and gave me a dreamy look.

Mike said, "Georgie's a little fuckin' crazy, but he's harmless." The older cop's name was George Alm, and he was the unit's prankster. I would later find out that Alm did this gay act to all the new guys who transferred into the unit. After the initial handholding prank, he laughed along with Mike and Lenny and then introduced himself: "Hey Pat, I'm George Alm. I was just fucking with you. So where'd you transfer in from, kid?"

"I just transferred in from the 12th District."

George then said, "Great! A ghetto copper *and* you're Irish; you'll fit in perfect here."

Over the years that I worked in Special Ops, George would provide many gut-busting laughs for me and the other guys, not only at roll call but also on the street. I remember once, after I had been in the unit for about a year, when Captain Walsh came down to do a pistol inspection at roll call, which was a rare event in the unit. The reason Captain Walsh was at roll call was because one of the cops saw an inspector checking personal vehicles in the parking lot to see if anybody had expired license plates or expired city stickers on their cars.

In Chicago, car owners have to buy a yearly city sticker for any vehicle they own. Cops were always getting caught driving cars with expired license plates or expired city stickers. Technically, by department regulation all units were supposed to have pistol inspection once a week. These inspections were hardly ever held in Special Ops, but with an inspector in the area, the captain was playing by the rules. Inspectors were part of a special unit; they held the rank of lieutenant and were given gold badges and wore white dress shirts. They rode around the city looking for cops to write up for minor violations, such as being off their assigned post, taking longer than the half hour allowed for lunch or dinner, or doing personal business while on duty.

At this special roll call conducted by Captain Walsh, he had everybody line up in several rows. When Walsh yelled, "Prepare for inspection," all the cops stood at attention. Walsh then said, "Ready for pistol inspection." All the cops drew their guns out of their holsters and held them at eye level. The inspection was to check all officers' weapons to make sure they were clean and also to check all officers' uniforms for cleanliness and their shoes shined.

Walsh walked down the first row of cops with Lieutenant Marcin at his side. When Walsh stopped in front of an officer, he would take his or her gun, look it over, and then hand it back to the officer, who reholstered it. He eyeballed the officer from head to toe, making sure their uniforms were clean and their shoes were shined.

When Walsh got to the second row, he was in for quite a surprise. There stood George Alm with his gun at eye level, his pants zipper wide open, and his dick hanging out. The captain just shook his head and moved on to the next officer as the room exploded in laughter. George would do almost anything to get a laugh, plus he had been in the unit for many years and was a top-notch street cop. The captain just expected and accepted George to be George, and he didn't disappoint.

Lieutenant George Marcin was the old-school cop—about 6'3", crew-cut hairstyle, and a deep gravelly voice—who conducted my first Special Operations roll call. When he entered the room, he walked right up to the podium in front of the room and yelled, "Okay, gentlemen, quiet down." He had to repeat himself several times before the room quieted down. Marcin read some general information from the C.O. (commanding officer's) book. This book contained important information updated on a daily basis; any new orders that came out were posted in the C.O. book. Also, information on any major demonstrations, recent crime statistics, and funeral information for any deceased officers (current or retired) was listed.

That day, Lieutenant Marcin said, "I have a special announcement. I want to welcome on board a new officer, Pat McCarthy, from the 12th District, into the unit." The room immediately erupted into catcalls, hoots, and howls. With a slight smile, he said, "Sorry, McCarthy, but your partner will be Officer Ray Blaa."

Everyone started clapping and making loud comments. One cop yelled, "Boy, did you get fucked, kid."

Ray stood up and gave everyone the finger, saying," Go fuck yourselves!"

It was all a big joke and you could tell by their reaction that these guys busted each other's balls all the time. The cops who worked in this unit were truly the most hardcore street cops in the department. They were special in many ways, but what made them stand out was the aggressive way they policed the streets of the city. These cops didn't take shit from anyone.

After the roll call ended, Lieutenant Marcin hung around and introduced me to several other officers in the unit. He said, "I've heard some good things about you, McCarthy, and I'm glad to have you in the unit." It was quite a welcome change from the greeting I received a little earlier from Captain Walsh. Marcin continued, "Sergeant Marty Joyce is your new supervising sergeant. He's a great guy; you'll really like him."

Sergeant Joyce walked up to me, smiling and smoking a pipe as he stuck out his hand and welcomed me to the unit. My first impression of Sergeant Joyce was that he seemed more like a college professor than a cop. He was very soft spoken and reserved. Sergeant Joyce said, "Let's go meet your new partner, Ray Blaa."

Ray was a short (only 5'6"), hard-looking guy with a ruddy complexion, piercing brown eyes, and a noticeable ugly scar on the right side of his nose. We shook hands as he said, "Welcome to Special Ops. You're going to love it here."

Ray was a well-known cop because during a violent demonstration at the 1968 Democratic National Convention that was held in Chicago, he was photographed whacking a demonstrator on the head with his billy club, or as they are sometimes referred to, a nightstick. The photo of Ray clubbing the demonstrator over the head appeared in newspapers and magazines all across the country. Sergeant Joyce told Ray and me to meet him at the Crystal Restaurant for a cup of coffee before we hit the street to work. The Crystal Restaurant was a rundown neighborhood greasy-spoon coffee shop at the corner of Irving Park Road and Sheridan Road. The Crystal restaurant was well-known for giving us a police discount, only charging police officers half the price of the actual bill, making it a popular place for the police to eat at and stop in for coffee.

Ray took me around the station, introducing me to several other officers and showing me around. I got my locker assignment from the unit secretary. Ray and I checked out a radio and a shotgun and headed out to meet Sergeant Joyce for that cup of coffee. As I strolled out to the parking lot, I carried a loaded 12-gauge shotgun and wore two handguns. I felt like a total badass ready to take on the world.

As Ray drove to the Crystal Restaurant for our meeting with Sergeant Joyce, he started to fill me in on some of the things I needed to know about my new assignment in Special Operations: "You'll find out pretty quickly that it's a lot different than working in a district, Pat. Most of these guys are hard chargers, and one thing about Special Ops is we don't take shit from anyone, and we also stick together."

I smiled and said, "It sounds like I found a new home." I told Ray about my not-so-welcome greeting from Captain Walsh.

He just laughed and said, "Oh, don't take Captain Walsh too seriously. Once you get to know him, he's really a good guy and a great boss. He's always got your back." Ray knew that I had to have clout to get into Special Operations—everyone who worked in the unit did—but he never asked me who my "Chinaman" was. After having several cups of coffee and shooting the shit for a little while with Sergeant Joyce, Ray and I hit the street for my first tour of duty in Special Operations. Ray said, "I've been looking for a suspect with a criminal warrant for his arrest on aggravated battery. Let's see if we can grab him today."

An "aggravated battery" charge is a felony in Illinois, usually related to a shooting, stabbing, or a beating in which serious injuries are inflicted. He told me that he had made several previous attempts to catch this guy but had been unsuccessful. Ray drove to a rundown apartment building on West Belmont Avenue, a poorly maintained neighborhood with various ethnic groups, which included many junkies and burglars. The area was also known for its large lesbian-gay-bi-trans (LGBT) population.

We parked behind the building and snuck in through the back entrance, which Ray seemed to know well. He turned off the police radio and motioned with a finger to his lips to be quiet. As we walked up a back stairwell, two ratty-looking drug addicts were hanging out there. Ray and I were in uniform, and by the look on their faces, you could tell that we had surprised the shit out of these two guys. We patted them both down for drugs or weapons and after finding nothing in our search, Ray said, "Get your sorry asses out of the building right now!" They were all too glad to be on their way.

We continued up to the third floor to apartment #302, where the guy who had the felony warrant lived. As we quietly stood in the apartment hallway, Ray whispered in my ear, "When I give you the signal, I want you to knock on the apartment door." Ray then got down on his hands and knees and looked under the crack at the bottom of the door. He then gave me the thumbs-up sign, and I knocked on the apartment door. I had no idea what the heck Ray was doing on his hands and knees crawling around on the filth stained carpet that covered the hallway floor. Ray again signaled for me to knock again. I did and there was still no reply from inside the apartment. He finally got up off the filthy carpeted floor and said, "Clearly, no one is in that apartment."

After several minutes, we left the building down the same stairway we had entered. After returning to our squad car and driving away from the apartment building, I began questioning Ray: "Exactly what were we trying to do at the wanted guy's apartment, and why did you get down on the floor to look under the door?"

He explained, "I wanted to see if the guy was home. When

you look under the space between the floor and the door, you can tell if anyone is in the apartment because people will usually come to the door and either look out the peephole or stand behind the door and listen. You can often see movement in the apartment if you look under the door."

I would use this technique many times throughout my career, especially in the older apartment buildings that dot the landscape of the city. Ray was right: people did give themselves away by approaching the door and peeking out or listening as they stood quietly by the door. You could often see some type of movement between the bottom of the door and the floor to indicate that someone was there but not answering the door.

I worked with Ray for a few weeks and learned an awful lot about working the streets. One day when Ray and I were out on patrol, I asked him about his nasty scar, which looked like part of his nose had been ripped off and sewn back on.

He said, "I was involved in a domestic altercation that turned into a violent fight. A drunken bitch literally bit a large piece of the right side of my nose completely off. The doctors had to take a section of my earlobe and attach it to the missing part of my nose to replace the chunk this drunken bitch had bitten off."

I asked, "So what happened to the bitch?"

Ray just gave me a sinister grin and said softly, "She definitely got hers."

I didn't ask Ray any other questions about the incident, but I'm sure the woman paid the price for scarring Ray's face for life. Most citizens have no idea how nuts and insane some people are when they're buzzed up and out of control on the street. Surprisingly, women can be some of the worst.

Over the years, I would meet other cops who were seriously bitten by people during altercations. I was bitten twice as a cop, but nothing as serious as losing part of my nose or half an ear. Once I was bitten on the hand; another time a burglar bit me on the forearm when my partner and I tried to handcuff him. I had bloody teeth marks before we could physically restrain him and get the handcuffs on his crazy ass. Both times, I was treated at the hospital and given a tetanus shot, but I didn't have any permanent scars like Ray had. There aren't too many jobs where people have to worry about shit like this happening to them in the normal course of doing business.

After a few weeks in the unit, I was assigned a regular partner to work with, Eddy Dickinson. Eddy was a few years older than me but still fairly new in the unit himself. This meant I would be working with a different squad and sergeant than when I was with Ray. My new sergeant was Ed Stack, a great guy and a very good, aggressive street cop. Sergeant Stack had been in the Special Operations Unit as a officer and had just returned to it as a supervisor after being promoted to the rank of sergeant. We hit it off right away and became good friends. Sergeant Stack loved police work and was always out on the street, working with the officers he was in charge of supervising. I loved it when he rode along with Eddy and me. It gave us another set of eyes and ears, as well as a backup officer if things got out of control or crazy, which happened quite often. Chicago can be a rough place to police, but the bad guys were a lot less likely to try anything when faced with three cops rather than one or two.

Chapter 9

Operation Snow Tow and Mayor Byrne

Handling unusual or "special" details was a normal part of being a member of Special Operations. During my time in that unit, I would be involved many of these details. While none were as unusual as "operation angel," which was discussed earlier, another unique detail I worked on became known as "operation snow tow." The Special Operations Unit was more than a ready force that could be sent into any part of the city for special situations; it was also a political tool used by the mayor and city hall at their discretion.

The weather forecast for January 12, 1979, was normal for a Chicago winter: up to four inches of snow accumulation over the next twenty-four hours. The snow started to fall around eight o'clock on the evening of January 12 and didn't stop until thirty hours later. The total accumulation was nearly twenty-one inches— the second largest snowfall in the City of Chicago's history. The worst had been the 1967 snowstorm that dumped a staggering total of twenty-three inches on the city.

During "operation snow tow," as it was referred to in the local newspapers, all Special Operations officers were assigned to work in four-man squad cars. I patrolled the 14th and 15th Districts with Bernie Jacobs, Pat Duckhorn, and Eddy Dickinson. Because of the massive snowstorm, the entire city was virtually shut down. City services, such as police and fire protection, were tenuous at best. Heavy winds and drifting snow left at least two and often three feet of snow on all the city streets, both main and side streets.

The first priority of the city was to clear the main streets so emergency vehicles could respond to calls for police and fire service. Working this detail was a unique experience for me. Our primary responsibility was to assist the districts' beat cars by responding to in-progress calls and show the public that the police department was still in control. The city was under a complete gridlock of abandoned cars. Because this storm dumped so much snow so fast, cars were often stuck in the middle of the streets. Our job was also to assist in getting the abandoned vehicles towed to parking lots cleared of snow. The biggest problem with this snowstorm was that there was no place to put the snow *after* it was plowed.

City officials launched the biggest cleanup effort ever to clear the streets and get the city back up and running again. Civilian companies were hired on as extra help to haul the snow that had piled up on the streets via dump trucks to staging areas, such as parking lots, golf courses, and parks in and around the city. There were also numerous power outages and garbage-collection issues to fix. We all worked twelve-hour shifts in the four-man squad cars. Very few people were out on the street, but that didn't stop the criminals from taking advantage of this unique opportunity to commit crimes, while having a distinct advantage of getting away with those crimes due to the unique circumstances the city faced.

The bad guys knew that the police had their hands full and there was a big increase in burglaries and thefts across the city. We chased thieves who were riding around the city on snowmobiles, committing numerous burglaries and thefts and quickly fleeing the scene. We were constantly stuck in the snow ourselves while still being tasked with helping ambulances dig out as they responded to emergency calls. Some of these included life-or-death situations.

"Operation snow tow" lasted about a week, and it was amazing to see how a huge snowstorm could literally shut down an entire major city for that long. Riding around Chicago in a squad car during the aftermath of this storm was like being on another planet—a really white one. The city had an eerie feel to it, as if we were working in Siberia, not the third largest city in our own country.

Only in a city like Chicago can a major snowstorm be the deciding factor in an important mayoral election. Michael Bilandic was mayor at that time, and his opponent in the Democratic primary was a savvy politician named Jane Byrne. The election was forecast to be an easy win for Mayor Bilandic. However, Jane Byrne was smart enough to use that horrible, unforeseen snowstorm to unseat Mayor Bilandic and take over city hall, making her Chicago's first and (to this date) only female mayor. Byrne ran TV commercials showing how inept the city's response to the major snowstorm actually was—and it worked. Little did I know at the time, but Jane Byrne's election as Chicago's mayor would have an interesting and positive effect on my police career.

≈≈≈≈≈

As I said, Mayor Byrne was an astute politician who had a number of unique approaches to running the city. Positive publicity for any mayor was always a good thing, especially when it related to the city's mounting murder rate, which was totally out of control in the late 1970s and early '80s. At that time, the Cabrini-Green Housing Projects (aka the Green) located on the west side were averaging approximately 100 homicides a year.

Mayor Byrne not only brilliantly used a massive snowstorm to get elected, she seized on another opportunity during her tenure as the city's first female mayor: to gain national and even some international attention, she and her husband, Jay, moved from a glitzy forty-third-floor apartment on Chicago's famous Gold Coast to an apartment in the Cabrini-Green Housing Projects. The mayor thought her presence in Cabrini-Green would bring much-needed national attention to the growing crime problems in the projects. Mayor Byrne also knew that her presence would ensure a massive police presence, which it did. For months, the entire Special Operations Unit was assigned to patrol Cabrini-Green. On the day the mayor moved into the Green, I was one of twenty cops who started work at 4:00 a.m. to ensure the building she was moving into was safe. Mayor Byrne personally greeted me and every other officer on that detail. She also sent $50 checks along with a card dated March 29, 1981, with the City of Chicago seal on it that read: "For all the brothers who were valiant. Thank You. Mayor Jane M. Byrne." I still have the original card and wish I hadn't cashed the check.

Even though it was said Mayor Byrne and her husband only occupied their Green apartment for just three weeks, it was rumored within the police department that she and her husband only stayed overnight in Cabrini-Green once.

Cabrini-Green consisted of twenty-three high-rise buildings and fifty-four two-story row-house buildings—crammed into just seventy acres of land. The projects buildings were a stark contrast to the gleaming, towering skyline buildings of downtown Chicago just a few short blocks to the east. Almost every building had burned-out apartments where you could see the blackened marks of scorched brick or concrete from the fires as flames once shot out of the windows. I remember my first thought when I started working the Green: *How could there be people living like this in a world-class city like Chicago?*

The entire area was littered with abandoned cars that sat about a foot off the ground on milk crates, missing tires and with all the windows and headlights broken or missing. The place really did look like a scene out of the movie *Mad Max*. There were very few patches of grass and dirt; most of the grounds were covered in concrete and asphalt with broken glass and garbage literally everywhere. The living conditions were about as bad as they could get, even when compared to those in a third-world country.

The sound of loud music blaring from passing cars and the big ghetto blaster radios that everyone carried around was constant, night and day. So were the gunshots that echoed throughout the projects. In Cabrini-Green the "shots fired" calls to the police were nearly constant. It was like being in northern Wisconsin during deer-hunting season. It was often impossible to determine where the shots were even coming from, unless it was nighttime and you were close enough to see the muzzle blasts. Much of the shooting took place between the buildings because different gangs controlled different buildings. You could live in one building and be part of one gang, and the building right next to it was controlled by a rival gang. The buildings' residents were controlled by gangs, and the area was one of the most dangerous in the country. The projects were in a state of total chaos all the time. Working in that environment as a cop was both exhilarating and mentally draining at the same time.

The Green was just several blocks from two of the most well-known neighborhoods in Chicago: Rush Street for its bars and night-life, and Old Town, which was a very cool and hip area of the city. If you visited Chicago as a tourist, there was a strong possibility you would go to the restaurants and bars on Rush Street. Old Town is the neighborhood where the famous comedy club Second City is located. Many of the best comedians in the country, both past and present, got their start at Second City.

The amount of violence and the lifestyles of those who lived in the projects were mind-numbing. I found the uniqueness of the environment almost addicting. As a cop working in that environment, you were always on edge; you had to be, to survive. Even the day shift was dangerous. I compare working the projects to riding a rollercoaster: it was balls out all the time.

One day, while working the Green, thanks to Mayor Byrne, my partner Eddy said, "Hey, Pat, let's get out of here for awhile. I need a break. Let's go see what the beautiful people are up to." I immediately knew what he meant: he wanted me to drive over to Rush Street and then take a nice cruise through Old Town before returning to the insanity of the Green.

I said, "I'm good with that," as I headed east down Division Street toward Lake Michigan. In just a few short blocks from the Green, Eddy and I were in a very different world—the one where the beautiful people lived and played. It felt good to relax, let our guard down for a little while, and put the violence and insanity of the projects behind us while we took a little break. I drove our marked squad car down Rush Street, checking out the tourists and the attractive residents all hurrying along. I then drove farther north and cruised back south on Wells Street, which is the main route through Old Town. Eddy and

I were shooting the shit while we sat in the traffic backed up from the stoplight at the intersection of North Avenue and Wells.

I first saw her out of the corner of my eye as she came running out of a narrow gangway between two buildings. At first, she was just a blur running toward our squad car, but then I noticed that her face and blouse were covered in blood. Her arms were in the air, waving frantically to get our attention. It was so surreal it almost looked as if someone were playing a prank on us.

As she got closer, I could see she was young, probably in her early twenties. Her screams of agony and fear pierced the air, and sheer terror was in her blood-soaked eyes. I immediately jammed the squad car into park and we jumped out. She kept screaming, "Help, help! Please help; he's still up there!" while pointing toward the gangway from where she had just come.

I grabbed her bloody arm and yelled at her several times: "What happened? Tell me what happened?"

She pulled away from me, hysterical and still pointing at the gangway, screaming "Please help; he's up there on the third floor and he's got my roommate! He was raping her when I walked in, and then he hit me in the head with a hammer! He's a skinny black guy; that's all I could see!"

I immediately got on the police radio and yelled, "Emergency, emergency; this is 4671 and I have a rape in progress at 1722 N. Wells. Third floor rear, male, black offender, thin build."

Eddy and I raced down the gangway toward the rear entrance of the building. Just then, we saw a shirtless black male leap across the gangway to the back porch of the apartment building next door. It was quite a leap, but this guy made it look easy. We immediately lost sight of the suspect, so I got back on the radio: "Squad, the suspect just jumped to the building directly south of my location."

Eddy and I ran to the back gate and into the alley, which is when we saw the suspect running south. I again got on the radio and said, "Squad, the suspect is running south through the alley toward North Avenue. He's shirtless and appears to be in his twenties." As Eddy and I gave chase, the suspect ran across North Avenue and continued south down the alley until he disappeared into a gangway. We were in hot pursuit of him as other officers responded to our emergency radio call. Eddy and I boxed the suspect in by relaying over the radio to responding units the suspect's approximate location. With the help of a Canine Unit during the search, the suspect was soon apprehended and taken into custody.

It was sad to see the physical and emotional trauma these two young female victims had to deal with due to the damage inflicted by this asshole rapist. So much for leaving Cabrini-Green for a little break in the craziness and violent crime atmosphere . . . .

Later in the day, I went to the hospital to interview them both about the crime. The story both the victims told me was that the one roommate, Karen, had left the apartment to pick up some items at the hardware store. When Karen left the apartment, she had inadvertently left the back door of the apartment unlocked. Her roommate, Mary, who had stayed back in the apartment, told me, "I was unpacking some boxes in my bedroom when I heard a noise in the kitchen, so I called out, 'Hey, Karen, that was fast. Did you forget something?'"

"That's when a black guy ran into my bedroom and started punching me in the face. He knocked me to the floor and started ripping my pants off. He then dragged me to the bed and raped me. As he was raping me, I kept pleading with him to stop, which is when I heard my roommate call out my name from the kitchen. The black guy jumped off me and ran toward the kitchen. I screamed, 'Karen, get out! Run!'"

When I interviewed Karen she said, "I was only gone for about a half hour, and when I returned, my roommate was screaming. That's when I saw the black guy run from Mary's room. I was shocked and asked the guy who he was, but he never said a word. He just grabbed a hammer that was on the kitchen counter and hit me twice in the head before running to the front room of the apartment. I ran down the backstairs as fast as I could to the street. That's when I saw your squad car and ran up to you to get help for Mary."

I'm happy to report that both victims recovered—at least physically. I attended several court hearings with both victims and a rape victim's advocate over the following months to secure a conviction of this violent rapist. He was convicted and, believe it or not, sentenced to only seven years in prison; he should have gotten seventy years. These two victims got a life sentence, because I'm sure there are many times in their lives when they are still reminded of that terrible day.

Chapter 10

THE AIRPORT

It was May 25, 1979, a warm spring day in Chicago. After a long harsh winter, everyone was ready for a change. The sun was shining brightly in a picture-perfect spring sky. I had lived in Chicago my entire life, and seen and heard many crazy things, but nothing could prepare me for the grief and sadness the rest of my day and night would bring.

I first saw the heavy column of thick, black smoke rising in the western sky and thought, *That must be one hell of a fire burning in the west side of the city.* Almost as soon as I noticed the thick smoke cloud, though, I heard the wail of emergency sirens going crazy. It seemed like every cop car, ambulance, and fire truck in the city was racing, lights flashing and sirens screaming, toward the rising smoke cloud. I tuned my car radio to a news channel and heard that a plane had just crashed on takeoff from O'Hare Airport. The initial reports were vague, but did not sound good. The radio announcer was only getting limited reports about what had happened at O'Hare. I would soon experience the aftermath of a horrific airplane crash for myself.

I was a Special Operations cop; I was supposed to be able to handle anything, regardless of how horrific it was. Fuck that bullshit. I was no different from anybody else—I was just as vulnerable and sensitive as any other human being. I have feelings and emotions, just like all people do, and if a cop tells you they aren't affected by what they see and experience, they are probably full of shit or straight-up nut jobs. Cops just learn to compartmentalize the insane shit they witness and have to deal with. I have no problem admitting that what I experienced at O'Hare that night changed my life forever. If I had felt any other way, I would be afraid that I might be losing my mind.

As soon as I pulled into the parking lot at Belmont and Western Avenue, the headquarters of Special Operations North for my next tour of duty, I instinctively knew that I was entering a world of police work that would probably change how I thought and acted for the rest of my life. Few people are required to deal with that type of intense level of stress and sadness that cops face over the course of their careers. Lieutenant George Marcin was standing outside in the parking lot, clipboard in hand, waving frantically as the Special Ops cops drove into the parking lot ready for their next tours of duty. Right away I knew some crazy shit was about to come my way because the lieutenant was never in the station parking lot with a clipboard in his hand; the stunned look in his eyes said a lot. That night would be the start of the most insane and disturbing month of my twenty-six years with the CPD.

As soon as I parked my car, Marcin hooked me up with three other officers and gave us a brief rundown: "This is a bad one, guys; it was a big jet that crashed." We immediately jumped into a squad car and headed out to the crash-site command post, lights flashing and siren blaring. The police radio was going crazy with nonstop chatter about the crash. It was rush hour and vehicle traffic was literally bumper-to-bumper, just crawling along at a snail's pace westbound on the Kennedy Expressway to the airport. We drove the entire way on the shoulder of the expressway. The officers I was riding with didn't know any more than I did about the plane crash or what had caused it.

One of the guys said, "You know we're going to be seeing some pretty crazy shit when we get to the crash site, right?"

Another officer said, "I can only imagine the cluster fuck we're about to get involved in."

All we knew at that time was that an American Airlines flight that had just taken off from O'Hare Airport had crashed, and that a lot of people had been killed at the crash scene. I would later learn that I was about to become involved in one of the darkest days in American aviation history. At 3:02 p.m. American Airlines Flight 191 took off from runway 32R at O'Hare International Airport, one of the busiest airports in the world.

The DC-10 was flown by Captain Walter Lux, a seasoned airline pilot with over 22,000 hours of flight time during his career. The first officer, James Dillard, and the flight engineer, Alfred Udovich, were also both experienced aviators, logging over 25,000 hours of flight time between them. As the doomed plane taxied down the runway for takeoff, parts of the aircraft's number-one engine began to fall off the wing. Eventually, the entire engine completely separated from the airplane and fell to the runway. The plane was able to lift off the runway and gain an altitude of approximately 400 feet before it nosedived into the ground killing all 271 people on board. Also killed in the crash were two people on the ground, who lived in a trailer park near the airport. The airplane was doomed as soon as the engine separated from the wing. The damage that was caused to the hydraulic system of the airplane was so extensive that the crew couldn't possibly control the airplane, no matter how experienced they were. To this day, American Airlines Flight 191 is still the deadliest commercial airliner crash in US history.

As usual for police officers, we were heading into the unknown. I had no idea what to expect, but I knew it wasn't going to be pretty. As we neared the crash site, we were directed to report to the command post that had been set up nearby to direct search-and-rescue operations. At the command center, groups of six were sent directly to the actual crash site two blocks away. I'll never forget the feeling I had as I walked toward the crash site. As a cop you're trained to handle many unusual and high-stress situations, but none of my training prepared me for this. The smell of jet fuel and smoke was overwhelming.

The burning wreckage had long been extinguished but smoke still hung in the air and eerily seeped from the ground. Police officers and firefighters milled around with dazed looks on their faces, all appearing to be in various states of shock. The size of the crash site was equivalent to about three football fields. It was total devastation. The first things I noticed were clothes and broken suitcases scattered throughout the site. When I first arrived at the crash site I expected to see an airplane broken apart on the ground, but very little of the airplane wreckage was even recognizable. It was just a twisted mess of burned and smoldering pieces of metal. It was hard to realize that what I was looking at had once been an airplane filled with hundreds of people.

The crash site was roped off with yellow crime-scene tape, and we were briefed on our assignments; we were told that it had already been determined there were no survivors. Everyone had been killed when the plane went down; it was sad and sobering to hear that grim news. We were directed to search the crash site for any evidence, such as body parts and personal identifications. It was a gruesome task to look for human remains, and I was immediately shocked by the number of body parts scattered throughout the crash site. You couldn't walk but a few feet without finding human remains; arms and legs and parts of human torsos were everywhere, most burned and badly charred. I couldn't help but think about all the lives that were going to be changed forever by this terrible tragedy. I tried to put those disturbing thoughts out of my mind as I collected body parts and put them in plastic body bags. It's the same feeling officers deal with at car crashes with fatalities; we see real people who often remind us of people we know and love.

Cops are constantly reminded of how frail and fragile life can often be. The amount of suffering, pain, and death average cops have to deal with during their careers can be overwhelming. Every year, approximately 400 police officers commit suicide in the United States, and I think a big factor in these suicides is the unbelievable number of stressful and heartbreaking situations we have to deal with on a regular basis.

As we slowly made our way through the crash site, collecting human remains, I came across what looked like a charred basketball on the ground in front of me. I bent down to get a closer look and was horrified when I realized it was a human head. After a few seconds I had to pick it up and bag it, but a cold chill traveled up my spine. Once part of a living, breathing human being just a short time ago, it was now just a burned piece of bone and flesh. At the west end of the crash site was a trailer park where two people on the ground had also been killed. We found some of the biggest pieces of airplane wreckage around this trailer park. We also found several bodies that were slightly burned, but mostly intact, wedged tightly under a pickup truck. We had to bring in a tow truck to raise the pickup enough to retrieve the bodies under it.

We also discovered a large piece of the airplane wreckage near-by. As we approached we could see what looked like a mannequin wearing a flight attendant's uniform. The body was fully intact and, for some unknown reason, was not burned at all. The flight attendant's face was covered by the wreckage, but the rest of her body lay on the ground as if it had been staged. I'll never forget the disturbing feelings I had that night. Many of the cops, firefighters, and other emergency personnel who took part in this disaster needed grief counseling after witnessing the aftermath of this tragic plane crash.

We worked the entire night under the din of portable lights and the constant humming of the generators brought to the site to help us search and recover bodies and body parts. I left the crash site early the next morning, mentally and physically exhausted. I went home and took a long hot shower, trying to wash the smell of smoke and jet fuel from my body. I hit the sack totally spent, mentally and physically. I couldn't believe that even after brushing my teeth and gargling with mouthwash I couldn't get the taste of burnt jet fuel out of my mouth. It took me a long time to finally fall asleep—the images that ran through my mind were hard to forget. I couldn't help but feel an overwhelming and deep sadness as I lay alone in my bed, replaying the horrible shit I had just experienced. I don't know how I fell asleep, but eventually I did, probably from sheer exhaustion.

When I awoke midafternoon on the next day, I called the Special Operations office to check in and get my assignment for that night. I was told that they were putting a detail together and needed ten volunteers to go back out to the crash site. It wasn't something I really wanted to do, but I was new in the unit and wanted to be known as a team player, so I volunteered for the special detail. Little did I know, but I wouldn't be through with the aftermath of Flight 191 for another grueling month.

I was told to report at 4:00 p.m. to an American Airlines hangar at O'Hare Airport. Upon arriving I was directed to a briefing room for a meeting. At the meeting, Lieutenant Marcin thanked us for volunteering for this duty and explained that we were assigned to assist the forensic experts brought in to identify the crash victims. We were also issued American Airlines photo identification cards to gain access to the airport and the hangar that was set up as a temporary morgue.

Seven refrigerated tractor-trailer trucks were brought in to preserve and hold the bodies and body parts. Forensic experts came from all over the world to assist in the identification of the crash victims. The Special Operations volunteers were responsible for retrieving the body bags from the refrigerated trucks and bringing them into the temporary morgue. The scene in the hangar looked like a movie set from a science fiction movie. Examination tables were set up with portable lighting and curtains to divide the tables and create a work place for the forensics people.

When the bodies and body parts were originally collected from the crash site, they were placed in numbered body bags. It was our job to go out to the refrigerated trucks and locate the body bag numbers, as requested by forensic people, and bring the bags into the hangar. They would then examine the contents, taking measurements and doing other forensic tests. When their work was completed, we would return the body bags to the refrigerated trailer. It was a gruesome job, crawling around a dark tractor-trailer truck with a flashlight looking for the number tags on the body bags. This same routine would be repeated over and over for the next month. I remember on one shift I worked where one of the cops lost his police badge in one of the trailers. We spent hours removing body bags from the seven trucks until we located the lost badge.

It was a long month of extremely tough duty. The other officers and I who took part in this detail received an award from the Cook County Medical Examiner's Office. The award was for taking part in a detail that went above and beyond the normal call of duty.

Chapter 11

On SWAT

Special Operations officers enjoyed many benefits and opportunities that others in the department didn't have. One of those opportunities was that we were eligible to become members of the CPD SWAT (special weapons and tactics) team. Becoming a member of a big-city SWAT team was a dream come true for me. When I was accepted into this unit in 1979, SWAT teams were a fairly new concept in police work. Having a specialized unit of highly trained and heavily armed police officers to respond to barricaded suspects or hostage situations was a novelty back then.

The department had what was known as the "war wagon," which stayed parked in a police facility near the center of the city. The war wagon was a truck equipped with SWAT gear, such as tear gas, shotguns, long rifles, and carbines. It also contained ballistic shields and battering rams, for knocking doors down, and other types of pry bars and forced-entry equipment. By today's SWAT standards, we had meager equipment to work with.

Two SWAT officers were assigned full time to the war wagon, which would be dispatched to the scene of any hostage situation or barricaded suspect. Other members of SWAT worked regular special-operations missions across the city until a SWAT situation arose. We were then notified via the police radio to respond to the war wagon, which would be located near the barricaded suspect or hostage situation. I really enjoyed the excitement and action I experienced in the six years I spent as a SWAT team member for the Chicago Police Department. I had many unique and challenging calls during that six-year period—ranging from the drunken husband or boyfriend taking a wife or girlfriend hostage, to a police officer being killed and a hostage being taken.

The things I enjoyed most about SWAT were the monthly training sessions and the camaraderie among our team members. When first assigned to SWAT, I was part of the containment-and-entry team. This means that when a situation requiring SWAT develops, the first priority is to seal the perimeter so the suspect(s) don't have a chance to escape. The next step is to try to establish telephone contact with the hostage taker. CPD had a policy that called for us to seal the perimeter and wait it out, unless hostages were being harmed. The suspects usually surrendered eventually and came out peacefully, even if they had already killed someone during the initial incident. During my time in SWAT, we trained hard on various entry tactics, while fine-tuning our shooting skills with rifles, shotguns, and handguns.

A certain set of rules and protocols had to be followed at the scene of a SWAT situation, such as: never let a suspect leave the perimeter we'd set up; never give drugs or alcohol to barricaded suspects; and never exchange a police officer for the release of hostages. I was on numerous situations over the years where we drew an imaginary line around the perimeter that the suspect could not cross. However, on some occasions, that line *was* crossed and we were told to hold our fire. The police brass in charge of these SWAT situations took great pride in the fact that the vast majority of these incidents ended without a shot being fired by the police, which is always the goal.

I joined SWAT to help people who were unfortunate enough to be taken hostage by criminals, not to make the bosses in charge look good. I eventually made my decision to leave SWAT due to a series of incidents, not just the cold-blooded murder of Officer Richard Clark (whom I knew personally) and another victim.

One summer night, while I was working a high-crime mission in the 15th Police District – Austin, the SWAT team received a call to handle a situation in which a mentally deranged man had shot and killed his mother in their home. Uniformed patrol officers responded to a call of "gunshots fired" at a home on the near-north side of the city. As they pulled up in front of the house, they were immediately pinned down by gunfire coming from within it. The responding officers took cover from the gunfire and set up a perimeter, and the SWAT team was immediately mobilized to handle the situation.

I, along with the rest of the SWAT team, was notified via police radio to report to a staging area near the scene. After an insanely wild ride through the crowded streets of Chicago, I arrived. By the time I got there, it had been determined that the suspect had shot and killed his mother, who was still lying dead with half her body protruding from the front door of the house. It looked as if she had tried to get out of the house when her mentally deranged son fatally shot her numerous times. It had also been determined early on that the suspect was alone in the house and did not have any hostages.

The commanding officers on the scene decided *not* to use tear gas to force the suspect out, because the type of tear gas used back then often caused fires. They decided that the best way to handle the situation was to try to talk him into surrendering peacefully. Due to the fact that no hostages were involved and a solid perimeter had been established, plus the fact that they had already made contact with the suspect by telephone and he was talking, it seemed like a logical plan. When the SWAT officers arrived, the original responding patrol officers took up defensive positions in the immediate area. The supervisors conducted a meeting at the war wagon by the scene, and they developed a plan for an officer to enter the house through a basement window. I volunteered to be that officer. I put on a flak jacket, which is a heavier bulletproof jacket designed to stop larger-caliber ammo, and armed myself with a shotgun from the war wagon.

The supervisor in charge said, "McCarthy, I want you to enter the house through a basement window on the south side of the building. It's already been pried open by other team members. Now

I'm *only* sending you into the basement as a forward observer to report any movement you might hear coming from the first floor so we can try to determine the shooter's location. If the suspect comes down the basement stairs, just climb back out the basement window."

I was totally flabbergasted by his instructions. I looked the supervisor right in the eye and said, "Are you serious?"

He answered, "Yes, I'm serious. Your job in the basement is only to inform the outside team members where the suspect is in the house if you hear him walking around."

I was still willing to go into the basement; that was part of my job as a SWAT team member. But I wasn't going to get shot in the back trying to climb out of that basement window.

I'll admit I was nervous (who wouldn't be?), but this is the type of incident SWAT team members in big cities and small towns all across the country are trained for. I made up my mind that if the suspect came down the basement stairs and he was armed, I would do what I had to do. Plan or no plan, I wasn't going to let myself get shot by anyone—especially by a mentally deranged person who had just brutally murdered his own mother.

As I made a tactical move toward the house I was to enter, I was notified by radio: "Standby. We're reconsidering the plan."

The hostage negotiator, who had been talking with the suspect over the telephone, told the command staff, "I'm making progress, and I think the suspect is about to surrender peacefully." As it turned out my insertion into the basement was called off, and the suspect did finally surrender a short time later. There were several other incidents that occurred during my time in SWAT that made me reevaluate my position on the team, but the incident that pushed me over the edge would happen years later.

Chapter 12

What It's Really Like

My first thought when I saw her running down the gangway between two houses was: *I can't believe how much she looks like my older sister, Eileen.* Her screams were those of total and complete anguish: ear-piercing sounds that are hard and scary to hear and digest. A cop has to react to those screams; it's our job. That's how crazy being a police officer can be at times. In all my years as a cop, that poor screaming woman stands out as one of the most distraught people I have ever witnessed. Maybe I feel that way because she looked so much like Eileen.

The woman was beside herself to the point that my partner, Eddy, and I could hardly understand a word she was saying. We were the first cops to arrive at the scene on the call: "two people shot" in a house.

I asked the screaming woman, "Can you calm down and tell me what happened here?"

She just kept screaming, "They're in the basement! They're both dead! Oh my god, oh my god! They're in the basement on the floor in the laundry room."

Other cops began to arrive almost instantly. My partner and I entered the back door of the house, guns drawn, without knowing what to expect or even where the victims were. We cautiously made our way through the house and noticed an open door, which led down a narrow stairwell to the basement. We slowly descended the stairs into a small, cramped basement. The ceiling was probably no more than seven feet high. Even though it was high enough to stand comfortably, it gave us the feeling we had to duck to walk around. Finally, we found them. They were both obviously dead; pools of blood framed their heads on the cold concrete floor of the basement laundry room. It didn't take us long to determine that this was a murder-suicide.

I never even learned the woman who resembled my sister's name because within twenty minutes Eddy and I were back out on patrol, hunting for bad guys, trying to erase the horror and sadness we'd just experienced. In Special Ops, we were always on the hunt.

Anguish

Fear

Pain

Disbelief

Anger

Mental Illness

Those are the sounds of different screams that cops hear throughout their careers. They come in many varieties and none are easy to hear, but as cops, we have to learn to deal with screams. Most gut-wrenching sounds stay with us longer than we'd like, and sometimes I can still close my eyes and hear those horrible screams. I know I will hear them again, at times, for probably the rest of my life. I still think of the victims and their families, especially when I watch TV newscasts or read about certain incidents in the newspapers. I've learned that this is just part of the job of a cop, much like combat soldiers who have experienced death and horror on the battlefield, but that understanding never made it any easier.

I've been retired from police work for many years now. My son, Ryan, is the fourth generation from my family to become a Chicago cop. He's just beginning to learn the true meaning of being a cop, and it really bothers me to know he'll hear many screams during his years on the force.

≈≈≈≈≈

The young kid was just walking home, thinking about what most kids think about on the way home after a night of hanging with friends in a nearby city park. All of a sudden, the quiet summer night on West Catalpa Street on Chicago's north side exploded with the sound of gunfire. The young teenager stood frozen in fear in the shadow of a big oak tree; the poor kid was too afraid to move as death and bloody carnage unfolded before him on a nearby porch. It was all over in a matter of seconds. No one should ever have to witness what this kid saw on that dark hot summer night. It was a murder scene that could have been right out of a horror movie. Three people gunned down in a matter of seconds while sitting on a front porch of a brick two flat building as they drank beer and shot the shit with each other.

When the gunfire ended it was eerily quiet for a few seconds, then suddenly an ear-piercing, blood-chilling anguished scream of a young woman filled the night air. The kid who witnessed this brutal triple murder started to run eastbound on Catalpa faster than he had ever run in his life. He just wanted to get away from the bloody murder scene as quickly as possible. As he ran toward the safety of his home, he told himself: *I'll never tell anyone what I saw tonight.*

He was going to lock what he saw that night away in the deep recesses of his mind, afraid that if he ever told anyone, the monsters might find out and kill him, too. But he didn't know that while he had seen the murderers, they had also seen him.

Three days later, the kid was again walking home alone after a night of hanging with friends. A car with two young Hispanic men slowly drove by, eyeing him menacingly. It didn't feel right, but he convinced himself that he was just paranoid and continued on his way home. About a block later, the car approached him again, this time from the rear. Suddenly, several gunshots rang out. *Holy shit,* he thought, *these guys are shooting at me.* He dove to the ground as fast as he could as several shots whizzed right past him. The car quickly sped away, leaving him scared to death and shaking with fear on the ground.

Just like the night of the triple murder, he ran home as fast as he could. This time he told his older brother, "I saw three guys shot and killed three days ago on the night the murders took place on Catalpa Street. I was scared so I didn't say anything, but two guys in a car fired several shots at me on my way home tonight."

His older brother yelled, "Are you crazy? You could have been killed! You should have said something about this right away." The older brother then immediately told their parents about what his younger brother had told him. That's when the story about the night of the triple homicide on Catalpa Street started to unfold. Until then, the triple murder was a big mystery, but now it wouldn't be a mystery for long.

The kid's father contacted the police and said, "My son witnessed a shooting several days ago on West Catalpa Street, and tonight he was shot at by two Spanish-looking guys who drove by him on his way home." The Gang Unit was immediately notified and soon it had a witness who would help break the case wide open.

That's how serial killer Fernando Zayas was finally taken off the streets for good. Gang specialists immediately interviewed the kid who witnessed the triple murder. The boy told Gang Specialists John Sebeck and Tony Audino: "One of the shooters looked like he was wearing a monkey mask. I saw two other shooters, but I only saw the face of the shooter who was closest to me. Every time that guy's gun fired, the flash from the shots being fired lit up his face in the dark."

When the triple murder on Catalpa went down, I was working the day shift. I clearly remember walking into work the morning after the murders; the office was buzzing with chatter. There was never a dull moment in the Gang Unit, but this morning seemed special. All the gang coppers were talking about the "triple" on Catalpa. Murders in the Gang Unit were a daily occurrence, but the triple on Catalpa took place in an area of Chicago that had very few gang-related homicides.

Every gang cop speculated about the murderer's identity. The talk ranged from a jealous lover to a crazy neighbor. Little did I realize that morning that I would spend the next forty-five days without a day off, working an insane number of hours—along with many of the other coppers in the unit—to put this triple-murder case together.

It all started many years earlier with the murder of a peewee member of the Maniac Latin Disciple gang known as Chi Chi. Fernando Zayas (aka Prince Fernie) promised to avenge Chi Chi's murder, and he eventually did with the triple murder on Catalpa. Fernie waited and longed for the day he would revenge the killing of his best friend, Chi Chi. Fernie and several peewee Maniacs had homemade tattoos that memorialized Chi Chi's murder: crudely etched in black ink on their arms, they read "Chi Chi RIP," which, of course means, "Chi Chi rest in peace."

The Maniac Latin Disciples had laid claim to a several-block area from Western Avenue on the east to California Avenue on the west. They also claimed and controlled the area from Division Street on the south to near Fullerton Avenue on the north. For a gang as vicious and powerful as the Maniacs, it was a relatively small turf, as Chicago gangs go.

The incident that led to the triple homicide on West Catalpa Street years later had occurred in the mid-1970s and began as just a schoolyard fight between two young teens. It ended with the brutal murder of three young men in their mid-twenties, who were gunned down on a front porch on a hot and muggy summer night in Chicago.

The fight started over some stupid argument that took place during a pick-up basketball game in a local schoolyard on the Maniac's home turf. Chi Chi and a young gang member by the name Miguel Vargas got into a fight over some bullshit. Vargas got his ass kicked by Chi Chi and left the schoolyard. Puerto Rican pride and a macho mindset was a big deal to gang bangers, even if they were only young peewees. Any slight embarrassment against a gang member was taken very seriously back in the day. Revenge for Vargas getting his ass kicked had to be dealt with.

Vargas left the schoolyard bruised and beaten up, but he wasn't gone for long. He returned a short while later and shot and killed Chi Chi. Vargas was arrested shortly after the murder and convicted for Chi Chi's murder in court. Because he was only sixteen years old at the time of the murder, he was locked up in juvenile detention until he turned twenty-one. It may sound crazy to normal citizens, but that was the law at the time. If a minor aged sixteen or younger killed someone, the system mandated release on the minor's twenty-first birthday. Miguel Vargas was released from jail when he turned twenty-one, and the Maniacs were waiting for him.

That was the reason the older gang bangers often used peewee members to do a lot of their gang hits. They knew that the system could only hold the minor gang members until they turned twenty-one. Many of the peewee gang members were more than happy to shoot and kill rival gang members. By doing a hit on a rival gang member, the peewee shooters would gain status and rank within their gangs that would carry over even when they were released from juvenile detention. When a peewee killer was released after turning twenty-one, he was back on the street with a strong ranking and big-time street cred.

Eventually, the criminal justice system realized how screwed up this was and they changed the law to allow prosecutors to charge juveniles—any kids under age seventeen—as adults. If Chi Chi's murder happened today, Vargas most likely would have done decades in prison, not just the few short years that he served.

While Vargas was locked up, Fernie Zayas became an active gunner/shooter for the Maniac Latin Disciples, and he eventually became its leader. A realistic estimate by Gang Specialists Billy O'Brien and John Howe, who were assigned to monitor the Maniac Latin Disciples for almost fifteen years, was that Fernie Zayas had either killed or was involved in the killings of eleven rival gang members.

He once shot a guy in Ray's Barbershop while the guy, whose gang nickname was "Worm," sat in a barber chair getting his haircut. Ray's was a neighborhood barbershop on North Avenue, just west of the corner of Western Avenue. Fernie put on a ski mask in the gangway next to the barbershop and, in broad daylight, calmly walked into Ray's and shot Worm in the head several times with a 9mm semiautomatic pistol, killing him instantly. As Fernie fled the barbershop and ran down the gangway next to Ray's to the rear alley, a young kid saw him as he took off his ski mask and ran away.

That young witness identified Fernie as the person fleeing the murder scene to the police. Fernie was then arrested and charged with this brutal murder. By the time the case went to trial, the young kid, who was the only witness, had been sent to Puerto Rico by his family to hide out. Everyone in the neighborhood, including the kid's family, knew he would never live long enough to testify against Fernie. Gang Prosecutor Ernie Di Bennedetto gave it his best shot in court to gain a murder conviction but without his only eyewitness, Fernie was acquitted at trial and free to kill again and again.

The investigation of the triple murder on Catalpa Street was in full swing after the witness to the murder picked Fernie out of a photo lineup. A photo lineup is when the police put a group of possible suspects' photos together and have witnesses view them. It all started to come together after the witness stated that the one shooter he saw clearly looked like he was wearing a monkey mask.

Fernando Zayas had piercing brown eyes that were intense and scary. He also had very distinctive monkey-like facial features, which made him immediately recognizable. A young kid could have easily thought the shooter (Zayas) was wearing a monkey mask, especially in the dark. Fernie once told my buddy Billy O 'Brien that he liked shooting people more than sex. How fuckin' sick and twisted could a human being possibly get? He stalked his victims like a predator in the wild that was hungry and eager to kill his prey. This man was the closest thing to a monster that I encountered in my twenty-six years as a cop: a cold-blooded killer who looked into his victim's eyes and smiled as he violently ended their lives.

Once the witness was located and he picked Fernie's photo out of a photo lineup, the game was on. The witness and his family were relocated from their home and out of the Catalpa Street neighborhood for their safety. Everyone in the Gang Unit and the Gang Prosecutions group in the Cook County State's Attorney's Office knew that one witness was not enough to convict Zayas; more proof of his involvement in the murders needed to be developed. Every cop in the unit was on the case; putting Fernie in prison was priority number one for not only the Gang Unit but also for gang prosecutions, which was a group of prosecutors assigned to prosecute only gang murders. These prosecutors were the best of the best in the State's Attorney's Office. When the Gang Unit and gang prosecutors worked together, magic often happened; the best cops working with the best prosecutors suddenly made many of the toughest cases not seem so tough.

Solving the triple homicide also needed a little luck, and one day that is exactly what we got. One of the Maniac Latin Disciples who was very close to Fernie was a gang member named Socorro Roldan (aka Coco). Socorro Roldan was shot several times by another Maniac gang member for violating the gang's rules. Fernie had a standing rule in the gang that no one was allowed to mess with the gang's dope business. The Maniacs were dealing a lot of cocaine on their turf, and Coco was one of the main dealers for the gang. The problem Coco had was that he started to use some of the cocaine he was given to sell. Fernie would give him several ounces of cocaine to sell but he would snort up some of it and then have to put in some type of filler to get the cocaine back up to the weight it was before he snorted some of it, which greatly reduced the coke's quality.

Fernie had warned Coco several times about using the coke he was supposed to sell. Fernie was all business when it came to the gang's dope-selling. He knew that if the Maniacs had the best dope on the north side of Chicago, they would make big money—money that the gang members, especially Fernie, could use for weapons, cars, and to party with. The money also came in handy when one of the Maniacs needed bond money because of an arrest. They also used the dope profits to keep a high-priced and very skilled defense attorney named Sam Adams on retainer and ready to defend any Maniacs who were arrested.

One day, Fernie decided to send a message to all the Maniacs who were involved in selling drugs for the gang. Fernie and several other high-ranking Maniacs held a secret meeting. It was at this meeting that Fernie told his fellow gang members that he was going to have Coco killed for constantly violating gang rules. Even though Coco and Fernie were very close for many years, the gang's business came first.

It was decided that Coco would be told that he was going to get a "head-to-toe, one-minute violation" as his punishment for breaking the rules. In gang speak, this meant that three gang members would take him into a garage and punch and kick him for one minute. Coco was allowed to cover up and block punches, but he was not allowed to fight back. As crazy as this might sound, that's what gang life was like back in the '70s and '80s. Most gang violations didn't end up with a gang member being shot; they usually resulted in a gang member being fined a small amount of money that would go into the gang's party money or being sent to a prison to take care of one of the gang's locked-up brothers.

Fernie wanted to send the strongest message possible to all the Maniacs: don't fuck with the gang's dope business. Coco's fate was sealed, and he had no idea what was about to happen, because, in his mind, Fernie was his brother.

Fernie told Coco, "The gang leadership has decided you need to be taught a lesson: no more fucking with the gang's cocaine business. Coco, I hate to do this but you put me in this position; tomorrow you're getting a head-to-toe, one-minute violation."

Coco reluctantly said, "Yeah, Fernie, I get it, and I guess I have to agree because I violated the rules." However, he didn't know the Maniacs's leadership had planned to kill him.

The next day Coco was escorted into a garage near the corner of Rockwell and Potomac Streets to accept his violation. One gang member held a watch and signaled for the one-minute violation to begin. The three gang members started to punch and kick Coco as he covered up the best he could. As the beating continued, one gang member, a guy named Ross, pulled out a .38 caliber revolver and shot Coco several times. After the shooting, everyone fled the garage, thinking that they had done their job and killed him.

Even though Coco was shot numerous times, he didn't die. He staggered out of the garage and started screaming for help. The police were called, and an ambulance took Coco to St. Mary's Hospital, where, surprisingly, he survived the shooting. While Coco recovered in the hospital, many CPD gang specialists tried to talk to him about his shooting. At first he played dumb and told the cops he had no idea who shot him or why. Gang Specialists Howe and O'Brien, who were assigned to monitor the Maniacs, knew differently; they had inside contacts in the Maniacs who secretly told them that Fernie had ordered Coco's shooting for violating the gang's drug-dealing rules.

Once Fernie's involvement in the shooting was known, there was a full-court press to get Coco to talk. My partner, Harry Fenner, and I visited him everyday while he was in the hospital. For some reason Coco and I hit it off, and I started to make some progress getting him to talk.

One day I said to him, "Listen, Coco, we know Fernie did the triple murder on Catalpa, and there's talk on the street that you were one of the other shooters."

Coco just smiled and said, "It wasn't me, bro."

It took several days and many long talks with Coco to finally convince him that his friend Fernie *had* made the call for him to be shot during the gang violation. It wasn't long before Coco became a full-blown informant and we got him to give up the critical information to help us crack the triple murder wide open.

Nearly everyone in the Gang Unit was trying to determine Fernie's accomplices when Vargas and the two other guys were executed on the front porch on Catalpa Street. To say the entire Gang Unit was consumed by this murder case would be a vast understatement. Many of the detectives from the Belmont-area Violent Crimes Unit were also working extremely hard around the clock to solve this triple murder. Even with all the hard work and many days we dedicated to this case, we were unable to nail down the names of the other two shooters. Several possible suspects were developed; they were picked up and interrogated but did not admit any involvement. We had our strong suspicions about who helped Fernie commit this brutal triple murder, but that wasn't enough to charge anyone besides him.

A street source told one of the gang cops that Fernie had been known to hide guns in coffee cans buried in his backyard. Armed with metal detectors, several gang cops descended on Fernie's backyard, after several hits on the metal detector numerous holes were dug in the yard. Nothing but junk and a rusted screwdriver were found. The same thing happened at Fernie's girlfriend Letty Sanchez's house, unfortunately with the same results. Then we got our break with Coco.

Coco's debriefing started when he was still hospitalized. As it turned out, he was going to be the one to bring Fernie down. After we gained Coco's trust and developed a unique bond with him, he started to openly talk to several gang state's attorneys and me about what he knew. Not only about the triple murder on Catalpa, but also the other unusual events that took place that night: the Maniac Disciples had held a celebration party that night. It was at that party that he and Fernie heated spoons on the gas burner of a stove and burned the homemade "Chi Chi RIP" tattoos off their arms. This ritual removal of the Chi Chi tattoos on their arms signified that Chi Chi's murder had finally been avenged after all these years. Coco also named the two other shooters in the Catalpa murders. Armed with the inside information he provided, several search warrants were executed in an effort to locate the three guns that were used in the murders; unfortunately, no weapons were recovered.

He even lured Fernie over to his hospital room that we had bugged and tried to get him to talk about the triple murder. I, along with some Area 6 detectives, state's attorneys from Gang Prosecutions Unit, and several gang cops, including our boss Commander Ed Wodnicki, set up a stakeout at the hospital, both inside and outside. We all had high hopes that Coco could get Fernie talking about the triple on Catalpa, and we were also interested in what he would say about Coco's violation and shooting.

Fernie showed up at the hospital under the watchful eyes of many cops and several prosecutors. It was an intense time, because as crazy as Fernie was, we had to be prepared for anything. Would he be armed and try to finish off Coco as he lay helpless in his hospital room? We planned for any possibility: I was posted in the lobby, pretending to read the newspaper off in a corner. My partner and Commander Wodnicki were staked out in an undercover car out on the street. Detective Bill Baldry was dressed as a doctor and hanging around in the hallway near Coco's room. We even had state's attorneys and some gang cops hiding in a broom closet next to Coco's room.

For all the excitement the meeting of Coco with Fernie generated, it ended without getting Fernie to say anything incriminating on tape. In fact, Fernie even denied he was involved in Coco's shooting: "Bro, you know I would never sanction a hit on you! I had absolutely nothing to do with you getting shot during the violation; Ross just freaked on you." Fernie seemed suspicious and only stayed in Coco's room a short time before saying, "I gotta go now, but I'll be back to visit you soon, bro."

As Fernie left the hospital, State's Attorney Ernie Di Benedetto said over the radio, "Let's take him down, guys." I immediately left the hospital lobby and was picked up by my partner and Commander Wodnicki as they pulled up in front of the hospital and I jumped into the backseat of their car. We still had eyes on Fernie as he walked west on Division Street and crossed Western Avenue.

We rolled up on him and jumped out of the car with guns drawn as Commander Wodnicki announced, "Fernie, you're under arrest for murder." I quickly put handcuffs on Fernie and put him in the backseat of the undercover car.

Fernie took it all in without showing any emotion; he just sat there and smiled. We drove him to the Area 6 Detective Division to be processed. The entire stakeout team met up there also. An attempt was made to interrogate Fernie, but he refused to talk, stating, "I want my lawyer."

The game was on. Now we had to prove Fernie's guilt in court. The trial preparations began immediately. Coco had an around-the-clock guard until he was released from the hospital a few days after Fernie's arrest. It was my job to hide Coco and make sure he didn't return to the Maniacs's hood. He was the key to convicting Fernie, and we didn't want to take any chances on losing him.

We decided to rent Coco a hotel room out near Midway Airport in Chicago, compliments of the State's Attorney Office witness-relocation fund. It was my job to pick up Coco every day and drive him to the State's Attorney Office, where, I, the other gang cops, and several state's attorneys conducted his debriefings to learn as much as possible about the inner workings of the Maniac Latin Disciples.

I also had to take Coco out shopping for dress shoes to wear when he testified in court. As odd as it sounds, he and I became really close. I even gave him a couple of my older dress shirts and a few ties to wear when he testified. The case eventually went to trial. Coco was our star witness, along with the young kid who saw the shooting that night. Fernie was convicted in 1983 and sentenced to "life without the possibility of parole."

In a strange twist of fate, Fernie won an appeal of his conviction in 1989, and the case had to be retried. The court kept Fernie behind bars, but it was a mad scramble among the Gang Unit and Gang Prosecutions to retry the case. It took a while to locate Coco, our star witness, and when we did locate him, he was doing time for robbery in an Ohio prison. Norfie Deceola, who was a retired cop working as an investigator in the State's Attorney Office, State's Attorney Lin Kowamoto, and I flew out to Ohio and convinced Coco to testify at Fernie's retrial. Fernie was convicted again and resentenced to "life without the possibility of parole." Fernie still sits in prison today, never to be set free to kill again. Ross the gang member who shot Coco was eventually convicted on a conspiracy charge and sentenced to decades in federal prison.

Chapter 13

CLOSE CALLS

Working street missions in Special Operations was exciting, but I also had a number of narrow escapes. One night we were working the 6:00 p.m. to 2:00 a.m. shift, called the "power shift" because most of the violent crimes throughout the city took place then. I loved working nights. The darkness, the shadows, and how people acted on the street, which was totally different than how they acted during the day shift, seemed to heighten the excitement of being a cop. During the day shift, many of the bad guys were still sleeping, or if they were out and about on the street, they weren't as aggressive or buzzed up on booze or drugs as they would be after the sun had set. As night gradually settled on the city, so did the violence. Usually things would be somewhat quiet until about 8:00 p.m.; that is when the city seemed to come alive with evil and violence, especially in the summer months.

Many people in the ghetto had no air conditioning, and on warm summer nights, they would be on their porches or just milling around out on the streets. Drinking and getting high on drugs seemed to be the favorite past times in these areas of town. However, with drinking and getting high came fighting and violence. The straight-up tension you could feel out on the street when patrolling the most violent high-crime neighborhoods in Chicago was why I became a cop, and I truly loved every minute of it. On a hot summer night in the ghetto, working as a street cop was one of the most exhilarating experiences anyone could have, outside of being a soldier in a war zone. You never knew what was around the next turn or what you would face on the next radio call.

One night, Sergeant Stack, Eddy Dickinson, and I were working a high-crime mission in the 23rd District, which at the time was located on the northeast corner of Halsted and Addison Streets on the north side of the city. The 23rd District was a melting pot of just about every ethnic group possible. Patrolling slowly, we passed by a white guy, who gave us a look that just didn't seem right. It's hard to describe, but cops develop instincts that normal citizens usually don't have or wouldn't even understand. Cops are trained to look for certain behaviors: the darting of the eyes, the look of fear and nervousness that criminals give off. It's like a primitive instinct that animals have, in which they can sense danger even though they can't directly see anything threatening.

As we passed this guy walking down the street, Sgt. Stack said from the backseat, "Let's talk to that guy!"

We circled the block and pulled up just behind the guy as he headed northbound on Broadway Street. As we got out of the squad car, we called out to the guy, "Police. Come here for a minute; we just want to talk to you."

He stopped walking and turned toward us with both his hands in his jacket pockets, but he just didn't look right.

I said, "Take your hands out of your pockets," as we walked up to him.

He started to slowly back away as we approached. Then, I heard the sound of two distinct clicks but didn't know what it was. The guy suddenly took off down the street running; we immediately chased him and caught up with him pretty quickly. He refused to take his hands out of his pockets and tried to pull away from us. The fight was on. I grabbed one of his arms and Sgt. Stack grabbed the other. As we wrestled with this guy, trying to pull his hands out of his pockets, I could feel something heavy in his right jacket pocket. It then suddenly dawned on me that he had a gun.

I started yelling loudly, "He's got a gun! He's got a gun!" I held his arm with one hand, and punched him as hard and as fast as I could about four times. We all fell to the ground in a heap. After a few well-placed punches to his kidney area, he went limp. We pried his hands from his pockets and handcuffed his hands behind his back. As he lay on the ground moaning that we broke his back, we found a small .22 caliber revolver in his jacket's right pocket.

When we went to unload the gun we recovered from the guy, we discovered that it was fully loaded and two of the bullets' primers were struck and dented but had not fired. The clicking sound we heard as we approached this guy was the gun misfiring twice as he tried to shoot us. I would have many close calls during my career, but this was definitely one of the closest. The only reason we weren't shot that night was that this guy was carrying around a fully loaded gun with bad ammunition.

I had another close call while in Special Operations, which occurred while my partner and I chased an armed robbery suspect armed with a fully loaded sawed-off shotgun. It happened one night when I was working "special employment." The City of Chicago had a program that hired off-duty police officers as a supplemental force to work on the Chicago Transit Authority (CTA), the local buses and trains that transported people throughout the city. Police officers could work one of their regular days off each week to earn extra cash on special employment. They were paid their regular salaries, and it was a nice way for officers to earn extra cash for a family vacation, to remodel a basement, or to buy a boat or motorcycle. It was officially called special employment by the city, but the cops called it "special enjoyment," because it gave them the opportunity to earn extra cash and most officers treated it as a day off.

When assigned to special employment, officers would ride the buses and trains as a deterrent to crime. The city would usually have over 100 officers per shift to cover the bus and train routes with the highest crime rates. Most officers worked this detail in uniform, but some officers worked in plain clothes. The plainclothes officers were usually picked from specialized units like Special Operations or Narcotics. I used to work this detail on a regular basis, most of the time in plain clothes, to pick up some extra cash. To me working special employment was a good time; I loved sitting on a bus or train, watching people when they had no idea I was a cop.

Some of the things we saw while working special employment were unbelievable. I remember one time I was riding on a bus on Clark Street with a Special Ops buddy, Bernie Brennan, when a professional shoplifter, wearing a long trench coat and carrying a shopping bag, got on the bus. Bernie and I sat apart from each other near the rear of the bus, watching this guy pull out different types of packaged meats from all over his body. He literally pulled out packages of steaks and sausages from his shirt, pants, and even his socks. He then placed these items in a shopping bag as if he were a bagger at a local grocery store. He had gotten away with his crime only to be caught by two off-duty cops working special enjoyment. We looked at the labels on the meat packages to identify the store and returned to it with our shoplifter in tow and under arrest.

Another unique case happened while working a bus route in plainclothes; I saw a guy eyeing all the passengers on the bus, looking for an easy theft mark. He had the distinct look of a predator eyeing his unsuspecting prey, looking for his next victim. As I watched this guy, I saw him spot an old lady, who looked to be in her seventies, get on the bus. As soon as this old lady sat down, he moved to a seat right next to her. The bad guy was carrying a folded newspaper, a tool that would help him steal from his unsuspecting victims without their knowledge.

This person was clearly a professional pickpocket, and he was quite good at it. He sat next to the unsuspecting woman and immediately went to work trying to steal her wallet from her purse. I sat back and watched this whole scene unfold right in front of me: the pickpocket used the folded newspaper held in his left hand to hide what his right hand was really doing. I could see him stretching and leaning against this old woman, while trying to reach into her purse draped over her right shoulder. I was shocked at how fast this crook was able to get inside the old lady's purse and remove her wallet. As soon as he had the wallet, he got up to get off the bus. When I saw him stand up to leave, I sprung into action.

I grabbed the pickpocket and said, "You're under arrest! I'm a police officer!"

Everyone on the bus turned to look at what was happening. Even my partner, Bernie, who was also on the bus, had no idea what was happening. I yelled out to Bernie as I grabbed the thief, "Hey, this guy just picked this woman's purse." I searched the suspect's jacket and found the lady's wallet in his pocket. I then said to the old lady, "Ma'am, this guy just stole your wallet from your purse."

Her response floored me: "Young man, you're obviously drunk; no one took my wallet!"

I then held up the lady's wallet and said, "Ma'am, I'm the police, and I just watched this guy take your wallet. Check in your purse for your wallet." It took a minute to convince her what had just happened and that I really was a cop as my partner and I handcuffed the very surprised thief.

When the old lady realized that her wallet was indeed missing, she said, "I'm so sorry, young man! I can't thank you both enough for catching this horrible person. My rent money is in my wallet, and I don't know what I would have done if he'd stolen it! God bless!"

It was a great feeling to know we stopped this rotten thief who preyed on vulnerable, older people. We called for a backup unit for transport and headed into the station to process our prisoner. I loved sneaking up on some rotten lowlife who preyed on easy marks. When we checked the thief's name on the station computer, we learned he had been arrested over ten times for theft and had done jail time in the past for the very same offense.

≈≈≈≈≈

One night when Bernie Brennan and I were working special employment, we were assigned to concentrate our efforts on the Clark Street bus line between Fullerton Street on the south and Devon Avenue on the north. When working plainclothes assignments, I used to carry a gym bag with my radio, flashlight, and handcuffs. About halfway through our tour of duty, we were headed northbound on the Clark Street bus. The bus was nearly empty and everyone looked legit, so I put my gym bag up to my ear and turned on the police radio to a very low volume to find out if anything was happening in the district where we were travelling. As I monitored the radio, I kept an eye on the front door of the bus, just in case any seedy characters got on. If anyone got on the bus that looked shaky, I would immediately turn off the radio and watch them.

I then heard a call announcing a robbery in progress at a tavern in the 4900 block of North Clark Street. The dispatcher also stated that a citizen had made the call after seeing the robbery in progress through the front window of the bar. The offender was described as a black male, approximately thirty to thirty-five years old, tall with a thin build, and wearing a long black-leather trench coat. The citizen who made the call also said the suspect was armed with a sawed-off shotgun.

I was totally surprised by the "robbery in progress" call, since we had just passed that tavern a second ago on the bus. We told the bus driver we were the police and to stop and let us off the bus. Bernie and I hurried off the bus and started to run southbound toward the tavern that was being robbed. Just a few doors away from the bar, we saw a black male in a long, dark-leather trench coat walk quickly out of the front door of the tavern and head eastbound down a side street. He never saw Bernie and me approaching as he fled the scene of the robbery. It was an unbelievable feeling, seeing the robber exit the bar right in front of us. We followed the guy as he quickly walked eastbound. Bernie was carrying a .45 semiautomatic pistol, and when we were about twenty feet behind him, Bernie jacked a round into the chamber of his gun.

At the time, the Chicago Police Department had a regulation that any officer who carried a semiautomatic handgun had to leave the chamber empty. Back then, semiautomatics were new in law enforcement, and officers were experiencing unintentional discharges, shooting their squad car windows or dashboards. We even had a cop in Special Operations shoot a radiator in the police station while playing with his new semiautomatic. The safety issues with semiautomatics were also questionable back then; some officers accidentally dropped their semiautomatics and they discharged.

Therefore, CPD decided that if officers wanted to carry semiautomatics, the chambers would have to be empty to avoid these types of accidental discharges. Officers could only chamber a round *when* it was needed. It was a common practice for inspectors to show up at roll calls and check on officers who carried semi-autos to see if there were rounds in the chambers. If an officer was caught with a round in the chamber, he or she would be written up and could face a day's suspension without pay. The department took these accidental discharges very seriously.

When Bernie jacked the round into the chamber of his .45, the sound of the slide going forward caused the perpetrator to look back at us. When he spotted Bernie and me following him, he took off running, and the chase was on. I was a fast runner, but the stick-up guy was also fast, and he started to pull away from us. The guy rounded a corner and ran down a dark alley. As I approached the alley, I slowed down a little because I didn't want to get ambushed as I turned the corner. I carefully looked around the corner down the dark alley but he was nowhere in sight, as if he'd just disappeared into thin air. I slowly entered the alley, looking for the location where the bad guy was hiding.

I looked around, trying to imagine what I would have done if I were in the bad guy's position. I noticed an open gangway at the rear of a large apartment building just off the corner, a place the bad guy might have disappeared into. I cautiously approached the gangway, straining to hear any sounds of movement or heavy breathing. As I proceeded down the dark gangway, I could hear Bernie running up behind me.

I was about halfway down the gangway searching for the gunman when all of a sudden from behind me, I heard my partner Bernie yell, "Freeze, asshole, and drop the gun!" As I quickly turned, I heard the sound of the sawed-off shotgun hitting the ground. I was stunned that I had just walked right past the perpetrator in the dark gangway. I don't know why he didn't shoot me as I walked past him in the dark. Bernie quickly cuffed the suspect. We recovered the shotgun from the ground and discovered that it was fully loaded. It turned out that the suspect had an extensive criminal record and was the type of criminal who would shoot a cop to try to stay out of jail. It was one more time in my career where luck was on my side. I gave Bernie a big hug and thanked him for saving my life.

My mom, Therese, and dad, Harry, on their wedding day.

My dad, Harry, and mom, Therese, with my siblings (left to right) Judy, me, Eileen, and Mike.

My Dad in his CPD uniform.

My dad, Harry (right), featured on the cover of the department magazine
helping an alcoholic.

My grandmother and my six siblings and me (first from right) at Wells Park.

My best friend, Mike Begley, in Vietnam.

Mike Begley (left) and me showing off our Marine Corps tattoos.

Me and my wife, Gail, shortly after high school.

Me and my partner, Eddy Dickinson, during Operation Angel.

Me and my partner, Janine Warner, on Operation Angel.

A very proud dad – Me and my son, Ryan (left), in tactical gear.

My Marine Corps photo – 1970.

Me in my CPD uniform, just after academy graduation.

Wearing SWAT Miles Gear. (top left to right) Eddy Mack, Sgt. Ed Stack, Ron Schultz. (bottom left to right) Me and Bill Campion. (Courtesy of Ed Stack)

At the FBI range, Great Lakes, Illinois.
(left to right) Everett "Bobo" Borders, John Boyle, Ed Stack, and me. (Courtesy of Ed Stack)

SWAT War Wagon (in background).
(top left to right) Ed Stack, Lenny Ciangi, me, and Frank Zingarelli
(bottom left to right) Wayne Frano, Eddy Dickinson, Joe Antosh, and Ralph Schauf.
(Courtesy of Ed Stack)

American Airlines I.D. card that was issued to me while working on identifying the crash
victims of American Airlines Flight #191.

The award I received from the medical examiner's office for my work on
American Airlines Flight #191

(left to right) Dan Sampila, me, George Ruckrich, Hiram Grau, and Pat Walsh.

(left to right) Bob Guthrie, Frank Radke, and Dan Sampila.

(left to right) Superintendent Leroy Martin, me, Maria Soto, Jean Learn, Jim Learn, Captain Joe Parisi, and Solly Vincent.

(left to right) Me, Superintendent Richard Brzeczek, and Eddy Dickinson
getting a department commendation.

Me holding an award that my FBI squad mates and I received.

Receiving an award in Shanghai, China (third from right).

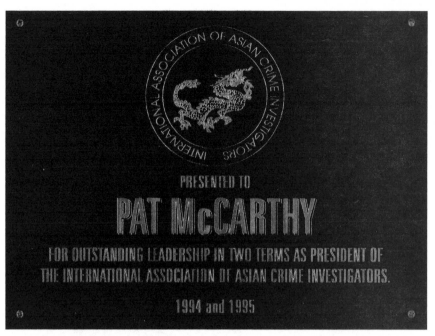

The plaque I received for my work as Two-term President of the I.A.A.C.I.

Professor Doug Daye (top row, third from right) and me (top row, second from left).
Carthage, Missouri, 1994.

Catherine Suh, serving life without parole for the murder of Robert O'Dubaine.
(Courtesy of Bill O'Brien)

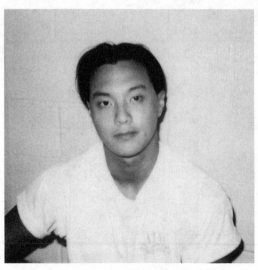

Andrew Suh, sentenced to 100 years for the murder of Robert O'Dubaine.
(Courtesy of Bill O'Brien)

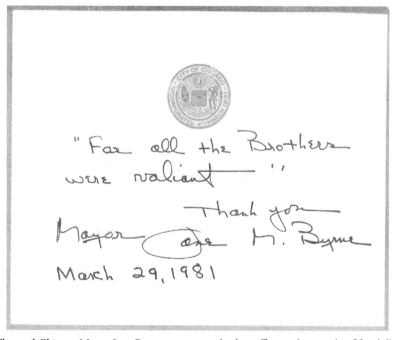

The card Chicago Mayor Jane Byrne gave me and other officers, along with a fifty-dollar check, for our work in the Cabrini Green housing projects.

My undercover photo – "Johnny Taylor."

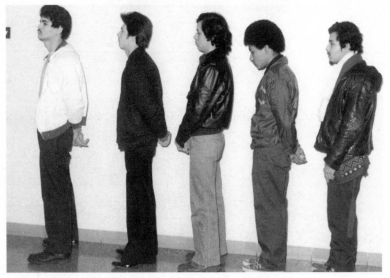

Fernie Zayas (second from right) in a line-up for the triple murder on Catalpa Street in Chicago. (Courtesy of Bill O'Brien)

A disguise I wore in court when I testified against gang members.

A disguise I wore in court when I testified against gang members.

(left to right) Pat Walsh, me, and Jimmy Learn.

Officer Richie Clark. (Courtesy of Erica Clark)

Det. Eddy Wiora (left) and me putting burglar bars on a Korean whorehouse.

Chapter 14

LADY D

When I looked at the photo, she was clearly dead as a doornail, wearing sunglasses with a cigarette hanging from her lips. I felt a little guilty, because I was the reason Lady D was killed—shot multiples times at close range.

I had first met Lady D about two months earlier. She was living in a dope flat with several real bad gang bangers. As long as I live, I don't think I'll ever forget that day. I had just parked my undercover motorcycle in front of a gang dope house on Leavitt Street a few blocks south of Belmont Avenue. The house where I was about to buy dope was run by a violent Chicago street gang known as the Insane Deuces. It was a beautiful, warm summer day in Chicago, the kind of day when I loved riding my department-issued motorcycle through the gritty streets of the city. I felt like a total badass. Bare-chested and shirtless, I loved the sensation of the warm sun on my face, chest, and back. I had on only a pair of dirty, well-worn blue jeans and a pair of boots. My .38 caliber chrome-plated snub-nose revolver was hidden in an ankle holster strapped to my left leg.

As I walked down the narrow gangway between two houses, I could hear Latin music blaring loudly from the backyard of the dope house. At the end of the gangway, I saw about ten hardcore gang bangers in the yard, listening to music, drinking beer, and talking shit. Suddenly, Lady D charged me at full speed out of nowhere. It happened so fast I didn't have time to run. I could see her fanged teeth as she clamped down hard on my ankle. As Lady D shook my leg violently, one of the gang bangers immediately ran up and kicked her hard, like he was a kicker on a pro football team going for a fifty-yard field goal, sending her two feet in the air. She then limped off whimpering into the corner of the yard and laid down. I was in complete shock and felt an intense uneasiness. *Did any of the gang bangers notice the gun strapped to my leg?*

I was so relieved when one of the gang bangers yelled, "Hey, sorry, bro. That bitch is crazy! Somebody is upstairs to take care of you."

I was breathing heavily as I climbed the long stairway to the attic apartment to score a bag of dope. I knocked on the attic apartment door and a gang banger I had bought dope from before answered. He knew why I was there and immediately asked, "What do you need, bro?"

I answered, "Hey, bro, I just want a half." A "half" was half gram of powdered cocaine, which was $50 back then. The gang banger reached into his pocket and handed me the bag of dope, as I handed him the $50.

I couldn't wait to get the fuck out of there. I hurried down the stairs and emerged from the enclosed stairway and back into the gang bangers' yard party where Lady D cowered in the corner of the yard. She had learned her lesson from the kick she took on my way in; she didn't dare move, but I felt a chill as our eyes locked for a brief moment. Lady D was a female pit bull and the mascot of the Leavitt and School Street faction of the Insane Deuces street gang.

My second encounter with Lady D was even stranger and just as intense.

Several weeks later, I again drove to the Insane Deuces dope house on Leavitt Street to buy more dope. This time no one was partying in the backyard, and everything was quiet as I walked down that narrow gangway. I opened the stairway door and started to walk up the stairs when suddenly I heard the distinct sound of nails scraping on wooden stairs, as if a dog were running down from the upper floor to get me. I knew right away that it was probably Lady D ready to take a second crack at me. I turned to run down the few stairs I had already climbed to get the fuck out of there. It was too late: Lady D was bounding down the stairs at full speed and ready to attack me. I grabbed a four-by-four piece of plywood that was leaning against the wall of the stairway and held it as a shield to block Lady D's attack. She went berserk trying to get at me as I held on to that piece of plywood for dear life.

I quickly backed down the narrow gangway until I reached the front gate still holding my plywood shield. When I got to the gate, I opened it and backed out, pushing Lady D away one last time as I quickly slammed the gate shut, but she kept barking and trying to get through the gate. I hurriedly ran to my motorcycle and rode over to the Lathrop projects and bought a bag of dope from some banger dealing on the street. That day was the last time I saw Lady D alive.

My crazy partners knew about my previous encounters with Lady D and shot her several times when she went after them during the execution of the search warrant. They thought it would be a nice touch if they took a photo of Lady D lying there dead with a pair of sunglasses on and a cigarette hanging from her mouth.My buddy that showed me the photo said with a laugh, "Who's the bitch now, bitch?"

I have to admit that while I did get a laugh from the photo, I felt a little sad that Lady D was killed. It was kind of a crazy ending to a successful drug operation.

Chapter 15

GANG CRIMES

I remember the very first time I saw a real gang cop working the streets. It was during the summer of 1978, and I was on the scene of a street shooting that had just occurred on North Avenue. As the Chicago Fire Department's emergency paramedics worked on the shooting victim, a dark-colored unmarked squad car pulled up to the crime scene and two guys got out, wearing blue jeans and sweatshirts; they looked cooler than shit. Both cops were wearing shoulder holsters with semiautomatics hanging from their chest-mounted shoulder rigs. It looked like a scene right out of a Hollywood movie. These two guys were the coolest cops I had ever seen on the street.

I asked my partner at the time, Eddy, "Who the fuck are those guys?"

He immediately said, "Oh, they're the badasses from Gang Crimes."

I couldn't take my eyes off of them as they walked around. Surveying the crime scene, they really did look like total badass, no-nonsense, straight-up street cops: you wouldn't want to mess with them.

As we drove away from the shooting scene, I said, "Eddy, tell me everything you know about the Gang Crimes Unit.

He said, "Gang Crimes is a small unit, and you need some very heavy clout to get in there. The reason it's such a highly sought-after assignment is that any officer accepted into the unit can be promoted to the rank of gang specialist, and you know how much that means!"

Gang specialist is the same rank as a detective, which was classified in the police department as D-2, meaning that gang specialists also received the higher detective's pay. Not only did they get detective's pay, they also always worked in plain clothes, no more uniform. After hearing Eddy describe Gang Crimes, I knew this was an assignment I really wanted.

As it turned out, I didn't go to Gang Crimes; the Gang Crimes Unit came to me. My undercover name was Johnny Taylor. I was an undercover cop, but not just *any* undercover cop: I worked as an undercover cop in the Gang Crimes Unit for five years—from 1984 to 1989.

≈≈≈≈≈

My time in Gang Crimes started in the early 1980s. Prior to the mid-1970s, a gang conflict was more like a scene out of *West Side Story*. Gang fights usually happened over turf wars for control of certain neighborhoods. Many of these early gang conflicts were over minor things, such as girls or a perceived act of disrespect toward a certain gang member. Most of these disputes were settled with fists, chains, car antennas, or other nonlethal weapons. It wasn't that gang members never shot each other before then, but the mid-1970s were a turning point in gang-related crimes because guns became much easier to obtain.

After her election in 1979, Mayor Jane Byrne, Chicago's new female mayor, decided to do something about the violent street-gang problem in her city. Gang shootings and gang-related murders were occurring at a more alarming rate than ever before. Mayor Byrne met with the top brass of the police department and came up with a strategy to combine the two most aggressive units of the Chicago Police Department, the Special Operations Unit and the Gang Intelligence Unit, into one elite unit, united to fight the growing street-gang problem. It became known as the Gang Crimes Unit.

Gang Crimes had three separate sections: Gangs North, Gangs

South, and Gangs West. Each Gang section was comprised of Special Operations officers and gang specialists. The members chosen from Special Operations were aggressive, seasoned patrol officers who worked in uniform most of the time, occasionally working special plainclothes details, and were known as the "tactical side." The gang specialists, though, always worked the plainclothes details, received D-2 detective's pay, and were known as the "investigative side" of the Gang Crimes Unit.

Unsurprisingly, when the two units first combined to take on Chicago's street gangs, some ego problems surfaced; these people were not used to working together. Roll calls became self-segregated: the investigative gang specialists sat on one side of the roll-call room and the Special Ops tactical cops on the other. At first, neither side trusted or liked the other. However, the die had been cast, and we were going to function as one unit—like it or not. I remember the bosses trying very hard to foster unity and camaraderie within the new unit.

Mayor Byrne assigned a respected and well-liked commander named Joe McCarthy (no relation) to head the new unit. Commander McCarthy's nickname on the job was "Patrolman Joe," because even though he was a commander, he was always working the streets with tactical officers from his district making arrests. This was very unusual because, usually, unit commanders never left the office—and when they did, it was to attend meetings, never to work the streets.

Joe McCarthy was a cop's cop. It was in his blood to patrol the streets and lock up bad guys, and he took a lot of heat because of it. The other commanders throughout the police department looked down on Patrolman Joe, but the rank-and-file cops loved him. He was one of us and was more than willing to mix it up with the bad guys, not just sit behind his desk in a safe environment, collecting a paycheck. Patrolman Joe was a unique boss and a strong motivator due to his reputation as a down-to-earth person and a hard-working street cop. When Mayor Byrne learned of the many street exploits of Joe McCarthy, she wisely appointed him to run the new, combined Gang Crimes Unit.

≈≈≈≈≈

The bosses, in an effort to create a better working environment, decided we should have a unit family picnic. When the idea was first proposed, it received a lukewarm response from both sides. The date for the picnic was determined anyway, and a picnic location in one of the city's forest preserves was reserved. The day of the picnic was picture perfect: a beautiful, sunny Chicago summer day. Families started to arrive, setting up their chairs and laying down blankets. Everyone seemed in good spirits, although the gang specialists and their families gravitated to one section of the picnic grounds, while the tactical officers staked out their own section.

The BBQ grills fired up and the beer started to flow. It started out slowly but after a short time, both groups started to mingle and introduce their families to other cops in the unit. The CPD Mounted Unit even had two horses on hand to give short rides to the kids. A K-9 officer and his police dog put on a demonstration for the group. As the picnic got into full swing, the families were into it and having a good time. One of the cops suggested a softball game between the tactical cops and the gang specialists. It sounded like a good idea, so a ball diamond was set up with homemade bases fashioned out of flattened beer cases. The tactical cops won the coin toss and elected to bat first. The families of both sides sat along the first- and third-base sides to watch.

The game only lasted one batter. Officer Pat Garrity was the first batter up; he stepped to the plate and swung at the very first pitch, lining a shot into the gap in right center field. As Garrity rounded third base, attempting to score, to everyone's horror, he barreled shoulder first into catcher Phil Szpicky, who was knocked on his ass. This set off a near riot as several gang specialists rushed to Szpicky's aid and began to push and shove Garrity, which started a free for all. It took a few minutes to get everyone calmed down as the shocked cops' wives on both sides gathered up their young kids and backed away. Needless to say, the game ended at this point. Both sides knew it was a bogus move by Garrity, who felt bad and apologized to everyone. It took some time but after things settled down, the picnic continued.

As odd as this may sound, the baseball incident seemed to bring everyone together. The one-pitch baseball game became quite a story, and somewhat of a legend, as word of it spread throughout the department. Over the course of time as both the tactical side and the investigative side of the unit got to know each other better, we became a tight and extremely effective unit.

≈≈≈≈≈

Gang specialist was a sought-after position— not only because of the prestige it carried, but because the pay level was higher. Only a few gang specialists, including me, did undercover work; the rest investigated shootings and murders, while also developing intelligence on the gangs they were assigned to monitor. Commander Joe McCarthy believed in rewarding his hard-working officers, so he instituted a policy that when a gang specialist opening came up, special consideration went to those within his unit.

Commander McCarthy had a small number of slots to fill at his discretion and when promotional opportunities existed, the jobs had to be open to everyone in the department. With 12,000 sworn members, CPD is the second largest in the country next to New York City, so competition was fierce for any promotions. When a D-2 test was given for new detectives, gang specialists, and youth investigators, thousands of officers applied. If I had to rely solely on my testing skills, I probably would have never been promoted to the D-2 rank. Back then, detectives, gang specialists, and youth investigators were all D-2 ranks, which entitled them to earn several thousand dollars more in pay per year than uniformed patrol officers. Today there are no gang specialists or youth officers; they are all classified as detectives.

Working in the Gang Unit for Joe McCarthy was great. We operated on a much different level than anyone else in the police department. We worked on gang-related murders and gang shootings, hunting down the worst of the worst hardcore gang bangers every day.

Commander McCarthy came to our roll call one day to address the troops: "You are all doing such a great job cleaning up the streets, and I appreciate your hard work. The streets of our city have become so unsafe that I'm declaring an all-out war on the gang bangers and instituting a new policy: I want all gang members to get a life sentence." Everyone in the roll-call room sat there confused and uncertain as to what he meant. McCarthy let his words sink in for a minute, then added, "We're going to give these assholes a life sentence one day at a time. I want these gang bangers locked up for any type of violation you can think of; I don't care how trivial the violation is. If these gang bangers are off the streets, they can't shoot anyone and they won't get shot."

These gang bangers were the worst of the worst, the most dangerous and most violent bad guys in the city; it was our job to make their lives miserable. Every cop in the Gang Unit went out every day to hunt down and arrest the worst of the worst.

We did what we were told and started to flood the lock-ups at different police stations around the city with gang bangers by the dozens. As we left roll call one night, one of the cops said, "It's time to go out and wreck someone else's life." That statement got a big laugh and could not have been more accurate. The Gang Crimes cops put hundreds of gang bangers in prison for decades; many were sentenced to "life without the possibility of parole."

It didn't take long for the ACLU to file a lawsuit against the CPD, though, alleging the gang bangers' civil rights were being violated by locking them up for congregating on the street, disrupting the flow of pedestrian traffic. There was quite a bit of heat over this ACLU lawsuit and, eventually, the mass arrests had to be discontinued.

≈≈≈≈≈

I always thought it was somewhat ironic that the Chicago mafia received a lot of news coverage and attention. It was always big news when some outfit (i.e., mafia) hoodlum got whacked. In reality, a mobster was only killed every few years, most often from a shot to the head up close and personal, usually with a .22 caliber bullet round. The dead body would usually be dumped in the trunk of a car often parked at one of Chicago's two airports: either Midway on the south side of the city or O'Hare on the far-northwest side. The dead body (or bodies) would usually be discovered when the stench of the mobster's rotting flesh was reported to the police as a suspicious odor coming from a parked car. In most of these instances, the car used to hide the dead body had also been stolen. It was a rare occasion for an organized-crime figure to be gunned down on the street—not that this never happened, but it was rare.

Meanwhile, the gang bangers were gunning each other and in-nocent bystanders down daily on the streets of Chicago. At the time, an outfit murder received major news coverage for days on end. Street-gang murders were barely mentioned—unless an innocent person, young kid or adult, was shot in gang crossfire.

As a tactical member in the Gang Unit, I was aggressive and made many quality, justified arrests. I worked with great partners and enjoyed the thrill of mixing it up with the bad guys on the streets of Chicago; it was something I felt born to do. I would have been a cop for nothing; getting paid to do the thing I loved most, hunting down bad guys, was a dream come true. I think my love for the job taught me the ways of the streets a little quicker than many other officers I worked with. I had a great desire to be the best cop that I could possibly be and I worked very hard at it.

Due to my successes on the street, I was recommended by sev-eral supervisors in the Gang Unit to be promoted to a gang specialist. The promotions board took their recommendations and meritoriously promoted me to the rank of gang specialist. It was an extremely proud day for me, not only in my police career, but also in my life. After all, how many people actually get to live their dream?

Making the transition from a Special Operations cop to a gang specialist was easy for me. I took pride in the fact that I could get along with almost anybody; I already knew most of the gang specialists in the unit and was accepted into their ranks without a hitch. When first assigned to work on the investigative side of the Gang Unit, I had several different partners. Typically, a new gang specialist rides with a team of partners as the third person in their car. It takes time for a permanent partner to be assigned.

Having a regular partner is almost like having a second wife. It has often been said in police circles that cops get to know their partners better than they do their wives or husbands. Due to the extended amount of time you spend together (eight hours or more a day, five days a week) and then consider the crazy situations you encounter during these extended time periods, you get to know your partner very well. After all, your safety and well-being may be directly tied to what your partner does or doesn't do in critical situations.

After being the third man on several different teams over a period of a couple months, I finally hooked up with a regular partner, Harry Fenner. Harry was a 6'4" full-blooded Native American. Harry was a good guy with a big heart who would do anything for anybody he knew. Not only was Harry a big person, but he also carried two guns. The movie *Dirty Harry* was popular at the time, and Harry wanted to be just like Clint Eastwood, who played the super cop in that movie. Dirty Harry carried a chrome-plated .44 magnum in his movies, and being starstruck, Harry Fenner bought the same .44 magnum with a six-inch barrel to carry on the street as one of his duty weapons.

Harry was considered a quirky character in the Gangs Unit, not only because of his chrome-plated magnum handgun, but also because he had strong Native American features and a ruddy complexion, which gave him a distinctive hard-boiled look. The first day we worked together, I brought Harry home for a brief stop to meet my wife, Gail. When I got home later the same night, I said, "It's been an interesting day, Gail. What do you think of my new partner?"

She answered, "Well, he seems like a great guy, but he *was* kind of scary looking."

I chuckled, and then I made a big mistake the following day at roll call by telling some of my buddies in the unit, "Gail said when she first saw Harry, he looked kind of scary," because from that day on, Harry became known as "scary Harry" throughout the Gang Unit. We became good friends and worked well as partners. We made quite a few great arrests and aggressively hit the streets every shift we worked together, developing criminal intelligence and confidential informants. Having a good CI, as they were known in police circles, was a big plus for any cop, especially for those in the Gang Unit. CIs are people on the street who became friendly with a cop and provided that cop with inside information that would normally not be known unless told to a cop by a street source/CI. Most CIs are developed after they're arrested for committing a crime and wanted to cut a deal with a cop to lessen their sentences or possibly not even be charged with a crime if the information they provided led to other arrests.

Spending that much time with a partner, often in life-threatening situations, can be difficult at times. The stresses of police work in a high-profile unit like Gang Crimes has been known to wear on a partnership. It was rare that partners stayed together for many years. In the mid-80s, after working together for about two years, Harry and I reached the point where we started to get on each other's nerves. Eventually we got what is known in police work as a "divorce." Harry and I parted company on a positive note, though, and Jimmy Learn became my new partner.

Jimmy was a Willie Nelson look-alike, with similar features and the same long gray hair and beard as Willie. Jimmy and I hit it off immediately. He had a sharp wit and said some of the funniest shit I have ever heard. He also liked to mix it up with the people we met on the street. Even though we were doing serious work, there was no reason we couldn't have a good laugh along the way, and we had more than our fair share. Jimmy and I were assigned to work in the Uptown neighborhood on the city's north side.

The Uptown area was a complete fucking zoo at the time. It had every type of criminal known to man, and then a few. Every ethnic group existed (and I mean just existed, not lived) in the Uptown area. The area was known in police circles as the "land of the lost," and it certainly lived up to its reputation. Wilson Avenue was ground zero for Uptown. Shootings, stabbings, and all-out brawls were as common there as dog shit in the park. If you lived in Uptown, it pretty much looked like the end of the road for you. At one time, Uptown was heavily populated with Native Americans, and it was sad to see a once-proud group of people in such dire straits; most of the Native Americans who lived in Uptown were alcoholics who roamed the streets like modern-day zombies.

Uptown was one of the few places in Chicago where you could rent a sleeping room for a few dollars a night. The area was dotted with liquor stores and small taverns, with a few low-end fast-food joints sprinkled in the mix. The apartments were small, old, and mostly shitty with dirty, moldy carpets and eighty years of filth and grime. Hot plates for cooking food were as common as stoves. Air conditioning was a luxury most Uptown residents had only heard about.

The area was also home to many street gangs that battled each other for control of a street or a corner to claim as their own. The predominant gangs were white-trash hillbillies, along with south- and west-side African-American and Mexican street gangs who had migrated to the Uptown area from other areas of the city. The conflicts were often brutal. Drugs were everywhere, and I understood why. If I had to live in Uptown, I would have wanted to take every drug I could get my hands on. The area was also home to many mentally challenged people who were warehoused in large apartment buildings—poor souls just waiting to become a victim of some street predator prowling the neighborhood.

The popular thinking at the time was to let these mentally challenged people live out in society, not in hospitals. The sad truth is that many people can't handle life on their own, especially in a toxic environment like Uptown. During the day, they were let out to roam the streets aimlessly, waiting for some dirt bag to take advantage and make them victims. Jimmy called it "airing out the cuckoos." It really was, and I think still is, a fucked-up way to treat people who can't live on their own. I know that compassionate, good-intentioned people came up with this idea, but if they'd seen the real truth, most would've been horrified by the results.

The Gang Unit was always trying to figure out how to get the upper hand on the gang bangers. Drugs started to creep into the gang lifestyle, along with the guns. It started out with the bangers smoking dope and using cocaine as recreational drugs, but escalated into the selling of both marijuana and cocaine. When the gang leaders realized there was a lot of money to be made selling drugs, they evolved into drug organizations and things on the street began to change dramatically.

Chapter 16

UNDERCOVER

If drugs changed the crime scene in Chicago, it was only natural for the Gang Unit to adjust and evolve as well. That's when my career took a dramatic turn, and I went from investigating gang shootings and gang murders to being one of the few gang specialists to become an undercover cop in the Gang Unit. I grew a beard, got the all-important earring, and off I went into the most challenging time of my career.

Buying dope from gang bangers was an effective way to get them off the street and sent to jail, where they belonged. I had many interesting experiences undercover; sometimes I worked alone, but I also worked with Officer Maria Soto, who eventually became the first female chief of detectives in the CPD. Maria and I put many bad guys in jail during the time we worked together, and I couldn't have asked for a better partner. Maria was bright, attractive, and a damn good cop. She also was Puerto Rican and spoke fluent Spanish, a big plus. Due to her light-brown hair and fair skin, you would never guess she was Puerto Rican or, even more surprisingly, an undercover cop.

Our boss at the time, Lieutenant Frank Radke, said to us, "Never let anyone on the street know Maria speaks Spanish. Make it your little secret so Maria can listen in on their Spanish conversations without their knowledge."

Having Maria with me seemed to make the bangers less suspicious about us. Maria and I frequented several different bars where the gangs dealt dope. Radke even got us a motorcycle to ride around on as part of our dope-buyers cover. With Maria on the back of the motor-cycle, we fooled a lot of assholes.

It was always funny how things played out when Maria and I went into these gang-infested bars in the Humboldt Park neighbor-hood. In the mid- to late 1980s, the Humboldt Park area had the high-est concentration of gang bangers in the city. We'd pull up to the bar on the motorcycle and have a few beers. The bangers couldn't wait to talk to Maria and eventually sell us cocaine. It never failed when Maria and I were in a bar having beers: as soon as I went to take a piss, the bangers swarmed her, trying to hit on her while I was in the bathroom. As soon as I returned from the bathroom, Maria had usually already made a connection and agreed to buy a couple bags of coke.

One of the best cases Maria and I worked was buying dope from the leader of the Assyrian Eagles street gang, Hotsa Saheim. He was a CI for Joe Rodriguez (aka Joe Rod), a good friend and one of the unit cops. Unfortunately for him, Hotsa was playing both sides: giving Joe Rod information on rival gang activity, while still dealing dope and doing shootings himself. Lieutenant Radke, our Gangs North boss, wanted to get Hotsa dirty in a drug buy so we could take him off the street. Maria and I had been buying cocaine from some of Hotsa's gang brothers on the street for several weeks. We had seen him around the neighborhood, but we were never able to buy dope from him so we could lock his ass up. With Joe Rod's help, we hatched a plan to send Hotsa to the joint; it was simple, but the odds of pulling it off seemed fairly remote.

Whenever Joe Rod contacted Hotsa to get information from him, they'd usually meet in a McDonald's parking lot on Lawrence Avenue just east of Kedzie Avenue. Hotsa lived about a half block away, just south of the McDonalds, and he always walked out the rear door of his house and down the alley to meet Joe in the McDonald's lot. The plan called for Maria and me to accidentally run into Hotsa in the alley when he was on his way to meet Joe Rod and try to engage him in conversation. I would tell Hotsa that we had been buying coke from his boys and I needed a couple of ounces for a trip I was taking to Florida in about a week. Maria would be walking our dog (really, my sister Judy's dog, Ellie), a super-friendly golden retriever.

The sting was set for a Sunday morning. Joe told Hotsa the day before that he would be calling him Sunday morning to meet and show him some photos of rival gang members so Hotsa could identify them. After a briefing with Lieutenant Radke, Joe Rod, and several other members of the Gang Unit, Maria and I picked up my sister's dog and headed over to Lawrence Avenue. We parked our undercover car nearby, got my sister's dog out on a leash, and waited for the signal to start walking down the alley for our encounter with Hotsa.

This was such a long shot; it almost seemed comical to make such a far-out attempt to get Hotsa. However, it actually worked even better that we had planned. Joe Rod contacted Hotsa, who told him he would be there in just a minute. We had a spotter watching the alley behind Hotsa's house. As soon as the spotter saw Hotsa walk into the alley behind his house, we were notified by a radio Maria had hidden in her purse. The game was on. Maria turned off the radio and we started walking Ellie down the alley. The timing could not have been better.

I said, "Hey, bro, how you doing, man?"

Hotsa looked at me, Maria, and Ellie and said, "Yeah, what's up? I haven't seen you in a while—since we were in county, man, right?" Hotsa thought he knew me from the county jail.

I was shocked, but I went right into my spiel: "Yeah, Hotsa—say, I'm glad I ran into you, bro. We're headed down to Florida next week, and I want to cop two ounces to bring down with me. You got anything?"

He immediately said, "No problem. Just page me and we'll work it out."

Maria quickly pulled out a pen from her purse and wrote down Hotsa's pager number. I shook his hand and said, "Great, bro, thanks. I'll give you a call in a day or two."

Hotsa said, "Cool, bro. We'll talk soon."

Hotsa walked away to meet Joe Rod, while Maria and I continued to walk Ellie down the alley. We both kept saying, "I can't believe that just fucking happened," over and over again.

When we were about a block away, Maria got on the radio to the team: "It's on. We just got Hotsa's pager number." Joe Rod met with Hotsa at the McDonald's and showed him a couple photos to cover the meeting.

Meanwhile, we met up with our backup team, including Lieutenant Radke, who said, "Great job, guys! Let's all meet up at the Blue Angel restaurant on Milwaukee and Foster."

I have to admit everyone was in shock that we pulled it off, including Maria and me. Maria jumped into another cop's squad and I headed to my sister's house to drop off her dog and raced to the Blue Angel restaurant to meet up with the team.

I remember Sergeant Danny Sampila just shaking his head in disbelief and saying, "I can't believe this hairbrained sting actually worked." Radke was so happy that he bought everyone breakfast. The trap was set. It wouldn't be long before the sting would be completed. We all felt confident that, in a short time, Hotsa would be sent to jail for several years.

Over the course of several days and numerous phone calls, I was finally able to arrange a deal for Maria and me to buy two ounces of cocaine from him. The deal was set to take place at the Golden Nugget Waffle House restaurant on North Lincoln and Montrose Avenues. Ironically, I grew up just down the street from this restaurant; my younger sisters Judy and Maureen had worked as waitresses there years earlier. I would have never chosen this location for the deal because I knew too many people in the neighborhood. It was Hotsa who suggested the Golden Nugget Waffle House, and I agreed because I didn't want to take the chance of spooking him.

Maria and I showed up at the restaurant about fifteen minutes early. I was on edge the whole time, afraid someone from my old neighborhood would turn up and burn the deal. We had a team of gang cops conducting surveillance on the location. While on surveillance, our team spotted Hotsa and another gang banger driving around the neighborhood, looking for surveillance. I'm sure that they were looking not only for cops but probably also for any sign of a "dope rip." A dope rip is when a drug dealer or a buyer is robbed of either their dope or their money. Robberies were a common occurrence in the drug world.

Eventually, Hotsa and his accomplice entered the restaurant, spotted Maria and me sitting in a booth, and joined us. They seemed nervous, but then so were we. After a short discussion, Hotsa asked, "So, do you have the cash, bro?"

I answered, "I'm solid, bro! Of course I got the cash. But do you got the dope, bro?"

He said, "Yeah, but I never do deals in restaurants. One of my boys has the dope in a car parked nearby. I'll do the deal with your lady around the corner, while you and my bro wait here in the restaurant."

I told him, "Sorry, bro, but I don't want to get ripped off, and I don't want my lady involved."

After going back and forth we finally agreed that Maria would stay in the restaurant with his friend, and Hotsa and I would do the deal in the car around the corner on Montrose Avenue. Hotsa didn't want to have the dope on him in the restaurant and must have thought that this would be the best way to do the deal. Little did he know that in a few short minutes he would be in handcuffs and on his way to jail.

As Hotsa and I left the Waffle House, I noticed Sergeant Bobby Biebel drive by in a covert car, so I knew that our backup was in place. Even if a rip occurred, I knew both Maria and I were in good hands. I couldn't help but think how many times that I had walked this same route as a kid, headed to Wells Park to play baseball. This was a much more serious game I was playing, and much more challenging.

Hotsa walked up to a car parked on Montrose Avenue and unlocked the driver's side door to let me in. As it turned out, Hotsa had lied about a friend waiting in his car. It was only us, at least for the time being. He seemed nervous as he pulled a paper bag out from under the seat, showing me that it contained two plastic bags filled with cocaine; each bag held an ounce of coke. I handed Hotsa the money and said, "Thanks, man. Good doing business with you, bro," as I got out of the car.

As most dope deals go, unusual shit always seems to happen that wasn't part of the original plan. The arrest signal was predetermined, but leaving Maria alone in the restaurant wasn't. I got out of Hotsa's car and began to walk back to the restaurant. Removing my baseball cap was the arrest signal to confirm the deal had taken place. I took two steps from Hotsa's car and took my hat off. The response was immediate; our backup team took Hotsa down before he knew what hit him, but I needed to check on Maria. By the time I turned the corner of Montrose and Lincoln, Hotsa's buddy was also in custody and being led away in handcuffs. They were both headed to the joint for a long time.

Maria and I couldn't have been happier. What started out as a far-fetched plan turned into a damn good case.

Sergeant Biebel said something to Maria and me that I cherish to this day: "That was a text book case you guys pulled off. I couldn't be prouder of you both."

I said, "Thanks, Sarge, but it was really great teamwork by everyone that made this work." It meant so much to Maria, me, and all the great coppers who took part in this deal. It was quite a compliment coming from Sergeant Bobby Biebel, who was a well-respected Chicago street copper.

Chapter 17

STICKS AND THE INSANE DEUCES

As the leader of the Insane Deuces street gang, I wanted Sticks real bad. Word on the street was that he once raped an eleven-year-old boy and then stole his bicycle. He was a complete animal. The boy and his family were so traumatized and intimidated by Sticks and his gang that they never reported the rape and bike theft to the police. Soon after this brutal incident, the boy and his family moved out of the projects.

I had met Sticks, who was a tall, skinny, black dude, a few days earlier in a seedy shithole bar located directly across the street from the projects. It wasn't a chance meeting. We knew Sticks hung out at that particular bar by the Lathrop housing projects on Chicago's north side, so a few Gang Unit members and I hatched a plan to get him. Sticks had his Insane Deuces gang brothers spread out, selling both pot and cocaine throughout the projects. Buying drugs undercover from gang bangers was a great way to take them off the street. It was almost impossible to beat a dope case when the buyer was an undercover cop. I had been buying cocaine from some bangers in Sticks's gang for several weeks.

Sticks was a street-smart gang banger, who was very cautious about whom he sold dope to—and he never sold dope on the street. His method of operation (MO) was to take over an abandoned apartment in the projects and deal from there, while his underlings exposed themselves to the dangers of selling dope on street corners. Believe me, selling dope on street corners opened up many dangers for the average gang dope dealer. Drive-by shootings by rival gangs occurred daily. The street dope deals also left the dealers exposed to police surveillance and arrests.

Sticks was street-smart, but he wasn't invincible—just harder to nail. I learned to love the thrill of buying dope from gang members; it was an intense and dangerous challenge. I had been doing this type of undercover work for several years before I went after Sticks and the Insane Deuces. I was a seasoned experienced undercover cop and felt up to the challenges and stresses associated with my job, but that didn't mean that I wasn't scared to death at times. Over time, I just learned how to deal with and control my fears.

When I first entered the bar across from the projects, I heard a loud commotion in the back by the pool table. A white female, who was obviously a junkie, was being slapped around by a big black guy she was mouthing off to. I knew Sticks was in the bar because a short time before I went in, two gang cops, Pat Walsh and Bob Ditusa, had checked it out for me and verified that Sticks was sitting at the bar. I walked up to the bar right next to him.

The bartender was focused on the black guy and the white chick he was slapping around, yelling, "Hey, knock it off you two, or leave right now."

Amazingly, the black dude stopped slapping the female junkie and settled down. I got the bartender's attention by loudly saying, "I need a six-pack of Old Style to go here!" I gave Sticks a quick glance and said to him, "Hey, bro, how you been, man? I haven't seen *you* in a while."

Sticks gave me a confused *Who are you?* type of look.

While I waited for the six-pack I'd just ordered, I yelled to the bartender, "Hey, man, get my buddy here a drink, and I'll take an Old Style with that six-pack." As we shared a beer, I engaged Sticks in conversation: "I've been copping bags of coke from your boys over at Hoyne and Diversey."

He nodded with a slight smile, like: *Yeah, those are my boys.*

I added, "Most of the bags I got were good, but I got shorted a few times."

Sticks then said, "I've seen you around the hood, bro, and I know you're a good customer. From now on, you can deal directly with me." He then wrote down his pager number on the cover of a book of matches and handed it to me, adding, "Shit is too hot on the street, but when you need coke, just page me, and I'll take care of you."

I shook hands with Sticks and said, "Thanks. My name's Johnny, and I'll call you soon, bro." I guzzled down the rest of my beer and paid for the beers and the six-pack to go. Nodding to Sticks, I left the bar with a spring in my step. *I've got Sticks on the hook; I just need to reel him in now.*

My undercover car was parked nearby, and as I got in to drive away, I saw Sticks standing in the doorway of the bar, watching me. I drove off to meet up with my backup at a predetermined location to fill them in on my meeting with Sticks. It was only a five-minute drive, but it gave me time to reflect on what just went down in the bar. A feeling of excitement, tinged with a little apprehension, swept over me. I watched the rearview mirror just in case I was tailed from the bar. I took a roundabout way to the meet spot, but saw no one suspicious behind me.

As I pulled into the parking lot, I noticed several Gang Unit cars parked off in the corner. All my apprehensions and fears drifted away as I pulled up, holding the matchbook with Stick's phone number written on it. I got out of my undercover car and pumped my fist in the air, matchbook in hand. I yelled, "I got that dog's pager number. He's fucked."

High fives and back slaps were exchanged among the group. Sticks was a big catch for the Gang Unit. It sure felt like we were well on our way to getting Sticks off the street. One of my buddies said, "Man, we're finally going to wreck that rotten prick! It's about time!" A nice jail cell for Sticks was what this operation was all about.

Several days after I met Sticks in the bar, my team decided

it was time to call Sticks and make a buy. I paged Sticks from a pay phone outside the Addison Street El station. This station is known as the transit stop for people going to Wrigley Field to watch the Chicago Cubs play baseball.

I tested the pay phone by calling the Gang Crimes office and asking Bernie Jacobs, the gang crimes desk officer, to call me back at this number. I just wanted to make sure that the pay phone was working and would accept incoming calls. The phone rang immediately, and it was good to hear Bernie's voice on the other end. I thanked Bernie and hung up the phone.

I thought, *Here I go again,* as I put my money in the pay phone and dialed Sticks's pager number. After two rings, I heard a beep, which was the signal to enter my phone number. I carefully typed in the pay phone number, making sure I did it right. I hung up the phone and waited, hoping Sticks would call me back soon. I leaned on the pay phone so no one would approach and try to use it. While I stood there, I thought about my wife and son, who were at home living a normal and happy life. I couldn't wait to get home later that night and be a normal human being again. I knew I was walking the edge, but I still loved it.

The ringing of the pay phone brought me back to reality. I didn't want to seem too anxious, so I let the phone ring two times before I answered with, "Hey."

Sticks responded, "What's up?"

"Hey bro, it's Johnny. I need an eight ball of cola." An eight ball is street jargon for an eighth of an ounce of cocaine.

Sticks then asked, "Are you in the hood now, man?"

I answered, "I'm on my way over there now. I can be there in ten or fifteen minutes."

"All right, bro. Do you know the project building just behind the parking lot facing Diversey?"

"Yeah, bro. I know right where that's at."

"Park in the lot next to the building and come up the back

stairway, the lock on the stairway door is busted, so it'll be open for you. Just go up to the second floor and knock on the door to apartment 207."

"I'm on the way."

I jumped into my undercover car and grabbed my police radio from under the front seat and called my backup team: "I just talked to Sticks, and he told me to meet him at apartment 207 in the building directly behind the parking lot facing Diversey."

One of my backup guys, Pat Walsh, said, "Good luck, Johnny, and be careful. You know that fucker is crazy." After double-checking that the police radio was turned off, I hid it under the front seat and headed for the projects.

To be honest, I was terrified. My mind raced and my heart was pounding a thousand miles an hour, just walking up the flight of stairs to Sticks's dealing apartment. I was afraid the very sound of my heart beating like crazy was going to give me away. I truly thought there was a very good chance I would be dead in a few minutes, or worse, that I would be taken hostage and tortured.

Here I am: a white boy in a mostly black and Hispanic, violent housing project. Who the fuck did I think I was? How was I going to get out of this safely? I had to convince myself I could handle this. I heard the deadbolt lock slide open, and as I braced myself for what was about to happen, I thought, *How did I get myself into this crazy shit? I should have listened to my closest friends, who told me I was "fucking nuts" doing what I did for a living . . . .*

As the door slowly opened, the dim light of the filthy hallway revealed a man with pure evil in his eyes. Seeing Sticks reinforced my feeling of dread. He motioned for me to enter with the movement of his head. As I entered the dark apartment, I squinted my eyes, trying to adjust to the darkness of the room I was entering. The small apartment was empty except for some garbage strewn around the floor. The only light in the room came from a streetlight that cast an eerie glow through a dirty bare window on the far wall.

The sound of the door closing behind me was like the sound of lightning striking the ground nearby. I tried to take it all in as fast as my mind could process the reality of this bizarre scene. A sinister-looking, shadowy figure in a dark-colored hooded sweatshirt stood in the shadows to my left. I slowly turned to face my fate, which seemed pretty uncertain at the time.

Sticks broke the uncomfortable silence as I entered the dark apartment by saying, "What's up, motherfucker?"

I swallowed hard and said, "Hey, bro, I'm here to cop an eight ball."

Sticks replied, "You packin', motherfucker?"

I responded, "I'm cool, bro."

That seemed to lessen the tension slightly in the room. I tried to stay calm and focused, bracing myself for what would happen next. *What if they searched me and found my gun?*

I was totally relieved when Sticks said, "Follow me."

Sticks walked through the shadows and climbed through a hole in the cinder-block wall that was about four feet high and two feet wide. I followed him into the darkness, accepting the fact that I was trapped like a caged animal. The feeling was one of helplessness and surrender. I felt the presence of the guy in the hoodie as he followed close behind me. The hole in the wall led into the apartment next door.

As I followed Sticks through the hole in the wall, all my senses were on high alert. I didn't know if I was being set up for a robbery or just following Sticks to get the dope I was there to buy. I knew my partners were expecting me to be in apartment 207, but I was now in the apartment next door to 207. If shit went bad, I was really on my own. I wasn't wearing a wire, so my partners had no idea what was going on anyway. I was relieved when Sticks reached into a pile of garbage scattered on the floor and pulled out a brown paper bag. He opened it and removed a plastic bag of cocaine. I already had my money in my hand. Sticks handed me the bag of dope and I handed him the cash.

I turned slightly to get my bearings and to see where the sinister guy in the hoodie was standing: he stood by the hole in the wall. I stashed the dope down the front of my pants as Sticks counted the money. I was expecting to go back through the hole in the wall and leave the same way I came in, but Sticks walked to the door of the apartment we were in and lifted a two-by-four board that held the door closed. He slowly opened the door, stuck his head out, and looked both ways up and down the hallway.

He then looked back at me and said, "Okay, it's cool, bro. Call me when you need more."

I said, "Thanks, bro. I'll hook up with you soon," and got the fuck out of there.

As I walked quickly down the hallway, a tremendous rush hit me. Once I hit the night air outside the project building, it felt like I could breathe again. The sounds of the night were great to hear. The hum of the traffic driving down Diversey and the city noise was music to my ears. I got in my undercover car and headed out of the projects parking lot to meet my backup team. I again closely watched my review mirror to make sure I wasn't being followed. It was a beautiful sight to see one of my backup cars fall in behind me as I headed north on Clybourn Avenue past the project buildings.

As I drove into the parking lot, which was located just about a mile from the projects, I was honking my car horn and flashing my headlights. I felt like a high school quarterback who had just thrown the game-winning touchdown. I got out of my car to high fives all around. Everyone was excited about what we as a team had just accomplished. It was a great team effort. We just ensured that asshole gang banger Sticks would be off the street soon.

Murphy's Law again came into play on this case. However, this time it actually gave us the break we needed to take Sticks off the street. Before we could indict Sticks on any drug charges, he was charged with the rape and attempted murder of a young girl.

The Insane Deuces gang had a party one night, and during this drug-and-alcohol-fueled party, a young girl was gang raped by several

179

of the Deuces. The girl struggled to get away and started screaming. The gang members panicked, and one of them strangled her until she went limp. They thought she was dead and fled the scene.

The young girl woke up a short time later, disorientated, but lucky to be alive. She contacted the police and Sticks and several other gang members were arrested and convicted. Sticks was sentenced to twenty-eight years in prison, a much longer sentence than he would have received for selling drugs to me.

Chapter 18

THE DAY OFFICER RICHIE CLARK
WAS MURDERED

The incident that caused me to resign from the SWAT team occurred on April 3, 1986, when veteran 19th Police District Officer Richard Clark was shot and killed on Chicago's north side. Officer Clark was working uniformed patrol at the time and was one of the first patrol cars to respond to a call of "shots fired" from a house on the 1300 block of West Lill Avenue. The first officers there were immediately pinned down by heavy gunfire coming from this house. Scrambling for cover behind their squad cars, Officer Clark took a quick look from his position. While raising his head to determine specifically where the gunfire was coming from, he was shot directly in the face with a high-powered rifle round, killing him instantly. A SWAT situation was called immediately, and all SWAT team members were summoned to the scene.

Before SWAT members arrived and took control of that incident, the 19th District patrol officers on the scene made a heroic effort to rescue Officer Clark as he lay shot in the face next to his patrol car. A brave group of his fellow officers drove a paddy wagon down Lill Avenue to use as cover; they came under heavy gunfire from the suspect and, at great risk to themselves, recovered the lifeless body of forty-eight-year-old Richie Clark. I've personally witnessed and have also heard about many heroic deeds performed by police officers all over this country, but the recovery of Officer Clark's body on Lill Avenue was pure heroism. Over the course of the next two days, the SWAT team sealed the perimeter and waited it out as negotiators did their job, talking this cop killer into surrendering.

When I'd first arrived at the scene, it was chaotic; police officers from the 19th District were in defensive positions all over the neighborhood. They were also in the process of evacuating the people in the homes near the scene. SWAT team members were instructed to set up a perimeter around the house where the suspect was holding an older woman hostage. At a short briefing at the rear of the war wagon, we were told that two people were already dead: Officer Clark and the owner of the building where John Pasch lived.

The incident began when the building owner got into a verbal argument with John Pasch about his past-due rent. The building in question was a small frame house with a basement apartment. Mr. Pasch lived in the basement apartment, and during the argument about his past-due rent Pasch shot and killed his landlord. Pasch then ran from his basement apartment and broke into the first-floor apartment right next door to his apartment, taking an elderly woman who lived alone in the apartment hostage. Pasch was wildly firing at the police from his neighbor's apartment. To show the cops he was serious, he shot the hostage's two dogs and threw their dead bodies through the front window of her apartment.

Already an intense scene by the time SWAT arrived, information was quickly developing about the suspect: we learned he was a gun nut and owned many handguns and rifles. The word we received at the scene was that the suspect was very heavily armed.

During SWAT situations like this, everyone is on highest alert. The SWAT team was sent in to take up positions to contain this incident, so the suspect had no avenues for escape. As a sniper at the time, I was positioned directly across the street from the house where the suspect was holed up and was assisted by Officer Ralph Schauf, a fellow team member. Officer Schauf and I set up a position in a gangway directly across the street to get a good shot at the suspect. As we anxiously waited for further information, we were contacted by radio and told,

"Contact has been established with the suspect, and he's talking to one of the department's hostage negotiators on the telephone."

Officer Schauf got on the radio to the command staff and asked, "Do we have a green light to take out the suspect if we can get a clear shot at him?"

The supervising officer in charge of the hostage incident immediately got on the radio and stated, "*No one* is authorized to fire a shot until further orders from the command staff. The suspect hasn't fired a shot from the house in quite some time and he's working with the negotiators, so we're hoping for a peaceful solution here."

I'll admit that for most officers on the scene, the last thing we were thinking about was letting a cop killer give up peacefully and just go to jail. We wanted to take him out the right way and still held out hope that that was how this incident would end, giving Mr. Pasch a shot in the head just like he'd given Officer Clark.

Intelligence had confirmed only one hostage; information was also relayed to us that the suspect was a crack shot and could shoot a deer at a full run from 100 yards. The actual number of guns the suspect had in possession was unknown, but we knew he owned numerous handguns and rifles.

As we waited for further information and instructions, we saw the suspect peek out the front windows of the house several times. The fire department's Special Equipment Section had brought in high-powered lights positioned to light up the front and back of the house. The whole scene looked surreal: almost like a movie set from some big Hollywood production. On several occasions, Officer Schauf told the bosses in charge that we had a clear shot at the suspect over the police radio. Each time he was told to stand down: no shots were to be taken by anyone unless ordered by the command staff. We were getting very anxious and anticipated that we would be given the order to shoot at any time—the bosses were just worried about the hostage getting accidentally wounded by an errant shot. Every one of the SWAT team, especially the snipers, was highly trained and could put a bullet within an inch of an identified target, and the *only* time a trained sniper will shoot is if they have a clear shot at a suspect.

Officer Schauf and I clearly saw the cop killer, Pasch, cautiously peering out from behind the curtains that dangled half in and half out of the broken front window of the apartment. We could have easily taken him out without harming the elderly hostage. It was extremely frustrating not being allowed to do the job we were trained for. *What if he eventually killed the hostage anyway? How would we feel if we could have ended this hostage incident by taking the suspect out as we had been trained to do in situations like this incident?*

After numerous attempts to get a green light to take this suspect out, Schauf and I were visited at our position by a SWAT supervisor who said, "Stay off the radio and make no further requests to shoot the suspect." Officer Schauf and I were really pissed off that we weren't allowed to do the job we joined the SWAT team for. *Why was I a trained sniper, then?*

To make matters worse, we found out that the suspect had broken off negotiations to watch a John Wayne movie on TV. Not only did they allow the suspect time to watch a movie, they even had a police officer risk his own life to deliver a pizza to the back door of the house so the suspect had something to eat. The insanity of the situation overtook me as I crouched on the ground in a gangway, freezing my ass off like all of the other officers at the scene, while this cop killer, murderer, and hostage taker ate pizza and watched TV. As bad as this sounds, it actually worsened as time went on.

At approximately 1:00 a.m. Officer Schauf and I were relieved by other SWAT officers. We were instructed to go home, get some sleep, and report back the next morning if the situation had not been resolved. I drove home in deep sadness with a heavy heart, thinking about Officer Clark and his family and the shock and pure grief they were experiencing. I also couldn't help but wonder how terrified the old woman must be, being held at gun point in her own home by a madman who had just brutally murdered two people. And here I was, going home to get some sleep while the poor woman was still there under those horrific circumstances. I knew that I wouldn't get much sleep that night with these extremely disturbing thoughts running through my head.

After a few restless hours of sleep, I immediately called the Special Operations office: "This is Officer McCarthy, and I'm calling to get the update on the hostage situation on Lill Avenue."

The desk officer said, "The SWAT situation is ongoing. You're to report to the command post set up in a Mexican restaurant just down the street from the scene."

When I reported into the command center, I was told, "McCarthy, you're being assigned with Sergeant Eddy Stack and several other officers to take up an assault position in the house just east of the house the suspect and the women hostage are holed up."

I had the pleasure of working with Sergeant Stack as a team member on his squad in Special Operations; I was happy that Stack would be calling the shots. The entire block had been evacuated by this time, and the command staff put an assault team together in the house next door, just in case a hostage rescue was warranted. I was proud to be a member of the entry team and kept thinking about the poor lady only a few yards away from us, probably hoping and praying we would safely rescue her from her jailer.

As Sergeant Stack and the other members of the assault team made a tactical entry into the house next door, I couldn't help wondering what the future held: *Would the hostage be killed if we tried to assault the house? Would I, or one of the other officers on the assault team, be seriously wounded or even killed?*

I would like to say I wasn't scared, but that would be pure bullshit. Outwardly, I put on a professional front as a tough SWAT officer. Inside, I worried about how this incident would be resolved. I tried to stay focused and positive because I was with some of the very best cops on the job. You couldn't ask for a better crew to hit a door with than these guys, but that was only a small comfort. I knew even the best-trained and bravest cops in the world could still die making a high-risk entry. After all, this suspect had already killed two people; he had nothing to lose at this point.

When we first entered the house next door, you could cut the tension with a knife. We were being called on to handle one of the toughest jobs in law enforcement: a SWAT entry with a cop killer and firearms expert holding a female hostage at gunpoint. The risks to your life in police work don't get much higher than this. We were in a complete stranger's house, armed to the teeth, and ready to execute a high-risk hostage rescue: it was surreal. We didn't know who even lived there. After entering the house, we examined both the front and back entrances. We needed to know the layout of both locations in case things broke bad and we had to make the assault. After assessing our options, we settled down in the front room of the home to plan our assault next door.

Sgt. Stack took control and made sure we had the equipment we needed. We were well armed with carbines, shotguns, and semiautomatic handguns. We also had a battering ram, various pry bars for forced entry, and ballistic shields and vests for protection. We discussed our positions on the team and how we would handle the entry. We also discussed that if we were called on to make the entry, we probably would have to kill the suspect. No one on the team had any problem with that. What did come up during our discussions as we waited for word from the command staff was the fact that we could have taken this cop killer out a long time ago. Not only did Officer Schauf and I have a clear shot at Pasch, but other SWAT officers also had good clean shots that could have ended this standoff the day before.

As we discussed the seriousness of the situation, one cop said, "Do you believe they actually gave that rotten prick a pizza?"

As we beefed and bitched like cops always do, a wide-eyed and obviously nervous supervisor came into the staging house said, "The hostage negotiations have just broken down, and the suspect is threatening to burn down the house. You guys need to gear up and get ready to assault the house," as he handed us gas masks to wear. The scene was extremely intense as we prepared to execute the assault.

Not many jobs require you to run into a burning building to rescue a hostage while some madman who had recently executed two people tries to shoot you. I found it ironic that we were asked to risk our lives because some no-balls supervisor was afraid to give the green light to shoot this hostage taker and cop killer a day earlier. In my opinion, this hostage situation was handled very poorly. As we anxiously awaited the word to begin our assault, I thought about my wife, Gail, and one-year-old son, Ryan. They were at home having a normal day as I nervously awaited the outcome of a deadly hostage situation.

As we checked our equipment, I studied the faces of my fellow SWAT team members. *Where they as frightened and unsure as I was?* If they were, they sure didn't show it. I was amazed at how professional and focused everyone on the team appeared. Sergeant Stack went over everyone's assignments, adding, "This is for real. Now if anyone has questions, this is the time to speak up." No one did; we knew what was at stake as we stood in a tight circle in the front room, waiting to make our assault. Several of us were assigned to charge the front door at the same time other cops were told to make entry to the rear.

We waited on high alert by the front and back doors of the house; if the word came down to assault, we were ready. After about twenty minutes of pure adrenaline rush and high anxiety, time seemed to stand still. That twenty-minute wait on high alert seemed like a lifetime; I silently prayed that everyone on the team would go home in one piece soon. Stack suddenly received word over the radio: "Stand down entry teams, Sergeant Stack. You got that?"

He replied, "Roger that."

We were informed: "Communication with the suspect has just been reestablished and he's once again talking to the hostage negotiations team."

The universal thinking with hostage situations was that if you could engage the hostage taker in a dialog and keep them talking, you had a good chance of talking them into surrendering. But that is not always the case.

After receiving the word to stand down everyone again sat down on the couch and front room chairs. You could feel the tension in the room slowly subside as we talked to each other. One cop said, "What a cluster fuck! Do these negotiators know what the fuck they're doing?"

Stack instructed, "Just stay cool, everyone; we still might have to assault. Apparently, the negotiators felt that the suspect is getting ready to surrender and release the hostage." This news was in sharp contrast to what we were just preparing to do. About ten minutes went by while Stack kept in constant contact with the command post. We then received the word we were all waiting to hear. Stack said, "The suspect has just agreed to peacefully surrender."

The situation changed real fast when Pasch released the old lady he had held hostage for two days and agreed to surrender. The entire assault team was very happy and relieved as we high-fived each other. It seemed too good to be true; we went from wondering if we were going to execute a very high-risk assault to planning how to handle the peaceful surrender of this dangerous cop killer.

Once the hostage was released, the entire dynamic of the situation changed. The suspect no longer posed a threat unless he tried something funny during his surrender. In situations like this one—with a guy who had already murdered two people, one of them a police officer—you can't take anything for granted. Sometimes suspects who are extremely despondent want to die, but they don't have the balls to kill themselves and will opt for the option of "suicide by cop." That means they don't have the nerve to kill themselves, so they put themselves in a position for the police to do it for them. Until the suspect is securely in handcuffs and in police custody, *nothing* is taken for granted. The surrender arrangements were the responsibility of the hostage-negotiations team. The terms of the suspect's surrender were negotiated, and he agreed to strip down to his underpants and walk out of the house with his hands held in the air.

Everyone at the scene was ordered to hold their fire, and the surrender came off without a hitch; the suspect did as he was told. A team of SWAT officers approached the suspect and handcuffed him. The bosses at the scene were nervous that one of the officers on the scene might want to seek revenge against the suspect. After all, he had just killed a well-liked and respected police officer. The suspect was immediately hustled into the house next door where we'd been waiting. As they hustled this cop killer into the house, the negotiating team immediately ordered the assault team to leave the house through the back door. It seemed that they, too, were worried that someone from the team might do something to exact revenge for Officer Clark's murder.

It was with great relief that I left that house. I didn't want to be anywhere near that asshole. It was a very emotional two days for the Chicago Police Department, but it was especially emotional for the brave officers who handled themselves so professionally during the entire incident.

The following day Sergeant Stack, another SWAT officer, and I resigned from the SWAT team. Stack had told me earlier, "Pat, I'm thinking of resigning from the team. The entire way this horrible situation was handled was just bullshit and totally against the rules."

I wasn't shocked to hear that Stack felt this way and said, "I know, and I feel like quitting myself. I'm having a hard time believing the bosses sent that rotten cop killer a fuckin' pizza and let him watch a John Wayne movie! What the hell?"

The real reason Stack and I resigned from the SWAT team was more than the fact that CPD had broken so many of its own hostage-situation rules. What really irritated me and the other team members I talked with was the fact that we could have taken this suspect out with a well-placed sniper round and ended the hostage situation on the first day. We knew that we did what all police negotiators strive to do: we waited for two days, hoping the suspect would surrender peacefully, which he eventually did. And we were lucky he did, because what if he had raped or murdered the old lady *after* we could have taken him out?

What if he had carried out his threat to light the building on fire and kill the hostage anyway?

We would have been forced to make the very high-risk assault and possibly gotten more police officers injured or even killed during the assault. Even though I really loved being a member of SWAT, I felt it was time to move on. They wouldn't give a SWAT team the green light to shoot a cop killer and hostage taker, and I didn't want to be a pawn in a deadly game of "Let's wait it out in every deadly situation."

It is true that this incident ended without further injury to anyone, but it certainly *could* have easily ended tragically for many people, including me, if things had turned bad. Our lives were unnecessarily put at risk. On April 5, 1986, I submitted my official resignation from the SWAT team, although I was still in a specialized elite unit. John Pasch was convicted and sentenced to death for two murders, but died in prison of natural causes in 1993.

Chapter 19

Sam's Bar and Little Man

During my time as an undercover cop, I bought a lot of dope in or around bars. One of the weirdest experiences I had in a bar happened when I was working alone. I had been buying heroin in a bar called Sam's; I remember the first time I went in there during the summer of 1986.

I quickly strode past the junkies and alcoholics who lined the bar, squinting my eyes to adjust to the dingy darkness of the place. It seemed as if every eye in the joint was focused on me, staring suspiciously. I brushed the looks off and thought to myself, *It's just because I'm a white guy with no shirt on. Just a piece-of-shit white boy with a frog tattoo on my stomach and a Marine Corps tattoo on my arm.*

Not many white guys ventured into Sam's. It was located on North Avenue where it intersects with Damen and Milwaukee Avenues. The clientele was mostly black and Hispanic, although no respectable black or Hispanic wanted to be caught dead in the place. It really was that fucked up of a bar: a shooting gallery for hypes, meaning people who injected heroin into their veins by hypodermic needle. It was also one of the last stops in life for the lowest-of-the-low drug addicts and drunks. I headed straight to the back of the bar because I had to take a piss real bad.

When I opened the men's bathroom door, I startled her. She was a black chick who looked about forty but was probably only in her twenties. Heroin can age a person very quickly.

I tried to act normal as she said with a sad voice, "Hey baby, how you doing, I'm almost done."

I replied, "No problem, girl, I'm just taking a piss."

I walked to the urinal and unzipped my fly. The situation was about as far from normal as about 99% of the people on this planet will ever experience. The girl stood over the toilet right next to the urinal and finished shooting heroin into the bulging vein in her arm. I stood there in total disbelief for what seemed like an eternity, trying to piss but, of course, it was difficult under the circumstances. I was relieved when the stoned-out black chick finally walked out back into the bar.

Sam's bar was a total shithole. The place was filthy and stunk of stale beer and piss. This was one of the most depressing and undesirable places in the world to have a drink, although you wouldn't know it by the volume of people constantly entering and leaving the place. Sam's was the last stop for many in a life of sadness and addiction. I thought: *This is as good as it was going to get for most of the people here. How pathetic.*

I was also buying heroin at the time from a rundown shithole apartment located at 2020 West Pierce Street—only a few blocks from Sam's. My connection there had just told me he was out of dope but was expecting a supply soon. So I walked over to the North Avenue bus stop in front of Sam's and took a seat on the bus stop bench, catching some sun with my shirt off. I had to take a piss, which is why I went into Sam's bar in the first place.

While I sat on the bus stop bench with no shirt on, two coppers from my Gang Unit, Jody Longos and Dave Sobcheck, pulled up to the stoplight. When they noticed me sitting there bare-chested, the looks on their faces were priceless. I had a hard time not laughing my ass off as Dave and Jody stared at me in disbelief—as if they'd just seen a ghost. There are many things I've forgotten about my undercover years; so much happened, and it all blends together sometimes. However, the black chick shooting up in the men's room at Sam's bar and the looks on Dave and Jody's faces are two things I'll never forget.

≈≈≈≈≈

Another unforgettable case was that of Daniel Pena (aka Little Man). One of the cops in the unit had been given solid information from a CI that Little Man was the driver of a recent drive-by shooting *and* that he hung out at a bar on North Avenue near Menard Street called Max's Lounge. It wasn't a lounge at all, just a seedy bar with a mismatch of misfits hanging out there.

Lieutenant Radke told me, "McCarthy, make it your mission in life to get next to Little Man and 'class X' his ass to flip him on the murder case." In plain English, he meant: "We want to force Little Man to give up the shooter by catching him in a drug deal." A class X felony meant that Little Man had to be caught selling a certain quantity of cocaine, which at the time was a little over an ounce of powdered cocaine. A class X felony conviction carried a sentence of six to thirty years in prison; even first-time offenders are not eligible for probation-only sentences and will serve prison time if convicted. Class X felonies also carry a fine up to $250,000.

I led the charge to hook up Little Man on a dope case to put some hardcore pressure on him. These asshole gang bangers thought: *Hey, I didn't shoot anybody, I just drove the car.* They didn't realize that they were just as guilty as the guy with the gun who did the shooting.

The game was on. I started going into the bar where Little Man hung out. It was a neighborhood joint: nothing fancy, but nowhere near the dive that Sam's was. What I usually did when I targeted a place to buy dope was go to the bar for a quick beer and then order a six-pack to go. I did this several times over the course of a couple of weeks. My plan was to be seen and give the impression that I lived in the neighborhood. This tactic was quite effective in establishing my presence there as "legitimate."

Eventually, Little Man struck up a conversation with me on one of my trips into the bar. He sat down next to me and quietly said, "Bro, I have top-quality cocaine if you ever need any."

I said, "Hey thanks, man. In fact, I'm headed to this chick's apartment in a little while, and I'd love to bring her a little 'present.'" I winked at him.

Little Man replied, "I've got quarters and halves tonight. How much of a good a time you wanna have?"

We both laughed as I answered, "Oh, I think a half would do it."

A "half" meant half of a gram of cocaine. Once again, the game was on. The trap was set; Little Man's days on the street were numbered, and he didn't have a clue. Over the course of several weeks, I made several other cocaine buys from Little Man.

It was now time to take Little Man off the street. One night while having a few beers with Little Man, I said, "Bro, I have a cousin who's looking to find a connect to buy bigger quantities of coke. His coke connect just moved out of town, and he's looking for someone who can deliver ounces of coke on a regular basis."

He instantly bit on this bullshit and replied, "Great, man. I can handle that for your cousin. My guy always has kilos."

I added, "All right, bro! We can both make a few bucks off my cousin," because I knew exactly what he was thinking. He could make some fast money by selling ounces of coke—in fact, a lot more money than he was making selling $25 or $50 bags.

I actually felt kind of sorry for the little prick, although I knew I shouldn't. I had to keep reminding myself that he was a rotten bastard who was willing to take part in drive-by shootings. It's still a weird feeling to look into someone's eyes, knowing damn well I was about to ruin his life.

After that encounter I told Lieutenant Radke, "Boss, I've got Little Man right where we want him! I told him my cousin was looking for a connect to buy ounces and he took the bait."

Radke smiled and said, "Pat, it's time to spring the trap on Little Man. Tell him you want to buy bigger quantities to sell to your cousin."

Several days later I met Little Man at the bar the day before his life would change forever. We had a few beers and Little Man said, "Bro, I just rented a new apartment, and I'm going to move in tomorrow. I've got some shit I want to take over there tonight, so can you give me a ride?"

"No problem, bro. Whenever you want."

"I've got a lamp and a box of clothes in my car. Do you want to go check out my crib now?"

"Sure, bro. Let's take my car."

We left the bar, and he went to his car and I went to mine. I pulled up next to his car and he loaded a lamp and a box of clothes into the backseat of my undercover car. As we drove to Little Man's new apartment, I asked, "Say, man, are you sure you can get me a couple ounces of coke to sell to my cousin?"

"Not a problem, bro. We can do the deal tomorrow."

"Great! I'll have the cash for you tomorrow."

Little Man directed me to his apartment, which was only about a mile and a half away from Max's Lounge. He was so proud to show me his new crib, a place I knew he would never spend a night in if all went well.

Once again, the trap was set. My backup team and I made plans to arrest Little Man after he delivered the cocaine to me the next night. Also once again, Lieutenant Frank Radke led the charge.

I met Little Man at 7:00 p.m. at the bar, like we had agreed upon the day before. Right away he asked, "Do you have the cash, bro?"

"I'm good to go, man. You got the coke?"

"I'll have the dope shortly; my supplier's just waiting on a delivery."

I ordered a couple of beers for us, and Little Man had no idea he was drinking one of the last beers he would ever have. As we drank our beers at the bar, Little Man suddenly got all serious on me. He knew me as Johnny, and he looked me straight in the eye. In a low, evil-sounding voice he said, "I know you're not a cop, Johnny, but if you are, I want you to know something: I'll kill you and everyone in your family, even your grandmother."

I was somewhat stunned, but I leaned back and said, "Go fuck yourself, man!"

He then gave me a sheepish but still threatening grin and said, "Hell, I'm just fucking with you, bro."

We sat there and drank several beers, waiting for his supplier to call him. I finally said, "Bro, I'm tired of waiting around. If you can't do the deal, I'll find someone else."

"No, man, I promise you the dope'll be here soon. Just waiting on the supplier, really!"

"Then page me when you get the dope. I have some shit to do," I said as I paid and left the bar. I drove away, watching my rear- and side-view mirrors to make sure I wasn't being followed. After driving a few miles making several turns and watching behind me, I knew no one was tailing me.

I drove a few more miles away from the bar and met up with my backup team. I could tell by the way a few of the guys were acting that they didn't think the deal was going to go down. I had my own doubts, but I had put a lot of time and effort into getting this little prick, and I was willing to wait it out. After a short meeting with my backup team, I headed back to the area where the bar was located and parked my undercover car a few blocks away; I wanted to be nearby when Little Man called. It took longer than expected but he finally paged me. I called him back at the bar's pay phone.

He answered excitedly, "Hey, I just got the dope, bro."

"Cool, I'll meet you back at the bar in about ten minutes."

I notified my backup team by radio: "The deal's on, guys. Little Man got the dope, and I'm headed back to the bar to make the buy."

My backup team and I had already planned how the deal would go down: I would tell Little Man that I didn't want to do the deal in the bar and that my money for the dope was in my car. I would lure Little

Man back to my undercover car and we'd take a short ride to do the deal. The plan was set up that once Little Man gave me the dope and I gave him the money, I would pump my brakes several times to let the guys know it was time for his takedown and arrest.

I got the dope and Little Man got his money, so I began pumping my brakes ever so slightly to signal it was "go time" to the team. Suddenly, lights were flashing from an unmarked squad car that had pulled up behind me and Little Man.

I said, "Fuck, bro, it's the cops!" I stopped the car and in an instant, Little Man and I were yanked out of my car and roughly thrown hard onto the hood of the unmarked squad car that stopped us. We were both handcuffed as our upper bodies and faces were very roughly slammed on the hood of the unmarked squad car.

I looked over at Little Man, whose face was only inches from mine, and said, "You rotten motherfucker, you set me up!" The look on Little Man's face was one of pure shock. Other backup team coppers were there in an instant.

I remember one of the guys, Ray Gueverra, yanked me off the hood of the squad car and marched me back to another unmarked squad car. Ray played it to the max, saying, "You piece of shit asshole; you're going to jail!" He literally threw me into the backseat of one of the unmarked squad cars for maximum effect as Little Man was marched to another squad and received the same treatment.

Both Little Man and I were driven to Area 5 Detective Division headquarters at Grand Avenue and Central. The guys played it out big time as Little Man and I were marched into the station with our hands cuffed behind our backs. Little Man and I locked eyes again as we were escorted into different interview rooms at the police station. I gave him an intense, cold stare of hatred; he just looked at me, still in total disbelief at what just went down.

Once I was away from Little Man in a separate interview room at the station, the handcuffs were taken off me. High-fives were exchanged with my backup team members, Lt. Radke included. It was an awesome feeling. I felt a rush of pure adrenalin that no drug can give you. I was proud and also thankful that I worked this undercover operation with the best coppers on the job. Now the real work began: getting Little Man to confess to being the driver on the drive-by shooting murder case we were investigating.

During Little Man's interrogation, he was told, "Pena, you just made a class X felony delivery to an undercover cop."

He was shocked and said, "There's no way Johnny is a cop."

Even though Little Man had threatened to kill me and my entire family if he found out that I was a cop, he still couldn't believe that I was an undercover cop. It was decided that I would go into the room where he was being interrogated. I had to show him directly me being an undercover cop wasn't just some bullshit story. So I borrowed a gun belt, holster, and gun from one of my backup guys and walked into the interview room where Little Man was being held. I walked up to him and grabbed him by the shirt, lifting him right out of his chair.

I looked him straight in the eye and said, "So you're going to kill my whole family. Is that right, asshole? You're fucked, dude, and you better wake up and realize it. You ain't killing anyone, asshole! You're on your way to fuckin' prison."

I then walked out of the room as Little Man just stared straight ahead, knowing it was over. A short while later, he confessed to being the driver in the drive-by murder. After he was convicted, Little Man was sentenced to fifty years in prison. As crazy as it may sound, Little Man died from a heroin overdose while serving his fifty-year sentence in the joint.

≈≈≈≈≈

Like all things in life, there is a beginning and an end. It was a sad day in early 1989 when my undercover career came to a sudden end. Maria, Jimmy Learn, and I were called into the Gangs office to meet with Captain Joe Parisi. The captain sat us down and said, "You guys have done some tremendous undercover work, but headquarters no longer wants the Gang Unit involved in undercover drug work."

We sat there in stunned silence. I didn't understand what kind of reasoning led to this decision. We were rocking and rolling on the street. As a unit, we were conducting undercover drug operations that were extremely successful. In fact, we were doing so well that many of our operations were being repeated a second time.

For example, we had successfully arrested and put a large number of the Maniac Latin Disciples, one of the most violent murdering gangs in the city, in jail. They were pitching dope all over their turf. The Gang Unit's first operation was a huge success and dubbed "operation pot-rock." This was an abbreviated term for the gang's main corner, Rockwell and Potomac, ground zero for the Maniacs.

After a successful operation, the Gang Unit would repeat the same process with another gang in a different part of the city. Another successful operation took place several miles from the Maniac's turf. This time we targeted the Latin Kings, who operated from the corner of Beach Street and Spaulding Avenue. The first operation we completed was given the name "operation crown-down." The Latin Kings's gang symbol was a crown, usually accompanied by the initials *L/K*. When a rival gang wanted to disrespect the Latin Kings, they would paint graffiti with an upside-down king's crown.

Both of those operations launched "pot-rock two" and "crown-down two." The second ones targeted the same gangs and took place after numerous members of each gang were indicted, convicted, and sent to prison for selling drugs to undercover officers. It never failed. There was always other gang members who would step into the jailed gang bangers' places and start selling drugs again on their turf. The reality was that there was too much money to be made in the drug business, regardless of the inherent risks. There was never a shortage of gang members ready to pitch dope for their gang.

When we questioned Captain Parisi about why the Gang Unit was being removed from the narcotics end of police work, he seemed uncomfortable and said, "The bosses downtown want the Gang Unit to only concentrate on gang murders and gang shootings."

I said, "Boss, you know that's bullshit! The undercover work we're doing, buying dope from the gangs, has a direct impact on the number of murders and shootings."

We all knew that the Gang Unit's undercover operations were responsible for putting hundreds of gang bangers in prison. It was a simple fact that if they were in jail they couldn't be shot or shoot someone else. To add insult to this bullshit edict from the downtown bosses, the shutdown of Gang's narcotics operations was effective immediately. We couldn't even clean up what we'd already had in play.

I told Captain Parisi, "But we have about twenty people we're about to indict at the grand jury. Why can't we finish that and then end our undercover operations?"

Parisi sadly shook his head and said, "Forget about any further work on the pending cases. Gangs is officially out of any drug-buying operations as of right now."

Maria, Jimmy, and I were furious. I said, "Boss we didn't risk our lives on these cases to just dump them like a pile of garbage."

Captain Joe (as Parisi was known) was a great guy, but he wasn't the kind of boss who wanted to make waves with the big dogs downtown. He then said, "The real reason we're being taken out of the narcotics business is that the head of the Narcotics Unit has been complaining to the superintendent about the Gang Unit's involvement in 'their' undercover drug operations."

I'm sure it was a jealousy thing, because every few months the Gang Unit's commander, Ed Pelinous, who was a publicity hound, would hold a press conference after a successful operation and arrest roundup. His press conferences got a lot of play on the TV news and also served to demonstrate that we were outshining the Narcotics Unit.

Jimmy, Maria, and I left Captain Joe's office in total disbelief. Not only were we out of undercover narcotics work, we were just told to forget about our months of hard and dangerous work and give up the drug cases we had already made. This was more bullshit than I could handle.

I immediately contacted my lieutenant, Frank Radke, and said, "Boss, I need to talk to you about what just went down, and I'm really pissed!"

In our meeting, Jimmy and Maria and I gave him the details of our meeting with Captain Parisi. I said, "Lieutenant, there's no way we're going to shit can the cases we've already made. That's just plain stupid!"

He agreed and immediately went over Captain Joe's head. I'm not sure who Radke talked to, but I do know that I was called into Captain Parisi's office the next day. He did an about face and said, "All right, you three can get the cases you've already made ready to be indicted. But after the last indictment, the Gang Unit will no longer be involved in any more undercover drug operations. That's final."

The bosses in police headquarters, or the "ivory tower" as it was referred to on the job, effectively shut down our highly successful undercover drug operations due to jealousy. I was happy that Maria was rewarded by being promoted to detective for her hard work on some dangerous and important undercover gang operations. Over the years Maria would be promoted through the ranks several times, making it all the way to becoming the first female Chief of Detectives—a major job in the CPD.

Chapter 20

The FBI Asian Gang and Organized Crime Task Force

My introduction into the secretive world of Asian gangs and Asian organized crime started in a subtle way. One day in August 1989, while still working in the Gang Unit, I was handed a "damage to property" case report by my lieutenant, Dan Sampila. The incident detailed in the report described a group of Asian gang members who had broken up a Korean nightclub with baseball bats. The Gang Unit was responsible for any gang-related activity, no matter the ethnic group. This "damage to property" case seemed a bit unusual; typically, we followed up on gang-related murders and shootings.

I contacted my "damage to property" victim, a Korean woman named Ms. Cho. After a short phone conversation, we arranged to meet face to face to discuss the incident at her nightclub. When I first met Ms. Cho, she was nervous, but seemed determined to have these gang bangers arrested. She knew they came from Chinatown and provided me with their descriptions and street names for a few of them.

As I listened to Ms. Cho describe how these gang bangers broke up her bar with baseball bats, I became increasingly fascinated. She went on say, "This gang has been extorting me for quite some time. I've been paying them $200 a week for protection at my bar, but I wasn't making enough money to keep paying what they demanded. When I told them that I could no longer afford to pay the $200 a week because my business was losing money, that's when the problems started."

As Ms. Cho and I continued to talk, she asked, "Do you know about the shooting that also recently took place in my bar?"

Surprised by that news, I answered, "No, I haven't heard anything, and I know nothing about it. What happened?"

"Well, one night a guy with a ski mask walked in and approached an Asian male customer who was drinking at the bar. Without saying a word, the guy in the ski mask shot the customer in the leg and then ran out of my bar." She added, "I'm sure that the property damage and the shooting are related. I feel like both incidents occurred to send me a strong message: 'Ms. Cho, you need protection, and only the gang can provide it, so pay up.'"

My mind was racing after hearing Ms. Cho's fascinating story. I asked, "How far are you willing to take this?"

Without hesitation, she answered, "I'll do whatever I have to in order to put these assholes in jail."

"Ms. Cho, you know you could be putting your life in danger if you cooperate with me and we go after these guys, right? I will protect you the best I possibly can, but I want to be totally honest with you about the risks." Then I asked her a question I thought for sure she would not agree to: "Ms. Cho, would you be willing to wear a wire and make some secret recordings of these guys?"

Without hesitation she said, "Absolutely."

I was thrilled that Ms. Cho had agreed to cooperate with the police. I also felt a little guilty at what might happen to her in the future. This is the real world of cops and bad guys. I was determined to make damn sure I could protect her to the best of my ability. I exchanged contact information with her and said, "I have to check something out, but I'll get back to you very soon."

I left the meeting with Ms. Cho with mixed feelings. I needed her help to investigate these gang bangers, but I didn't look forward to the responsibility of protecting her 24/7. I knew those gang bangers would not hesitate to kill her if they ever found out she was cooperating with the police. Little did I know that this meeting was going to have a major effect on both of our lives. We were about to embark on a unique journey together, ready to go toe to toe with some of Chicago's most secretive and violent groups: Chinese gangs, Vietnamese gangs, and Asian organized crime groups.

I'd like to say I was totally confident and that I knew we could pull this off *and* keep Ms. Cho alive. That would be total bullshit, however. I had grave doubts and concerns about the future when I started to think about what could go wrong.

When I went back, I told her, "I can get the protection money for you from the Gang Unit's petty cash fund. When I give it to you, we want you to contact Kojack (the street name of the extortion group's leader) and tell him you got the message and will start paying the $200 a week again like you used to."

We had Ms. Cho set up a payment for the following Saturday in a second-floor room above her bar. The meeting for the payment was made, and the plan called for me to hide between an inner and outer wall in a space about two feet wide as a witness and try to record the extortion payment with a small handheld tape recorder.

On the Saturday night of the first reinstated extortion payment, two Asian gang members showed up at Ms. Cho's bar to collect it. As directed, she led the two gang members up to the second floor of her nightclub; she then left the room to get beers for the gang bangers. It was a pretty cool feeling as I looked through the air vent and held the small recorder to record what they were saying as they waited for her to return. Then I watched in horror and disbelief as the two Asian gang bangers stood up and pulled guns from the waistbands of their pants. They were showing each other their guns when suddenly they both then pointed these guns directly at me, pretending to shoot. *How could they possibly know that I'm secretly watching them?* I thought as stood on a chair hidden between two walls in total darkness. I was peering through an air vent, waiting to get shot; it seemed as if they were toying with me.

How the fuck did I get myself into another crazy mess? It's over; you're probably a dead man.

What was only a matter of a few mind-numbing seconds seemed like an eternity. I wanted to flee but had nowhere to go. I was trapped behind a wall in a dark, cramped, and musty space on the second floor of a Korean nightclub—trapped like a rat in a cage. I wanted to scream, *Please don't shoot me! I surrender. I give up. I promise I'll never tell anyone what I just saw*, but I luckily knew enough to keep my mouth shut.

Suddenly, the door to the room opened up and my informant walked back into the room, carrying a tray with several bottles of beer. The Asian gang bangers quickly tucked their guns back into their waistbands and sat back down on the couch. I could barely breathe as I stood on a chair frozen in fear. I felt light-headed and nauseous as my mind tried to process what had just occurred. Ms. Cho sat down in a chair next to the couch, put the tray of beers on a small table, and calmly resumed a conversation that had started ten minutes earlier.

I had a hard time keeping still and maintaining my balance, standing on an old metal chair as I watched through the air vent near the ceiling. My knees were shaking and my breathing was deep and erratic as I waited to see what would happen next. Ms. Cho was cool and collected, though. I secretly watched a rare site: Asian gang members in the process of extorting an Asian business owner.

She slowly counted out the $200 I had given her and handed it to one of the gang members. He quickly tucked the money into his pants pocket as Ms. Cho promised to make another payment next Saturday. The gang bangers then got up and left the room, followed by Ms. Cho, who turned to look up at the vent I was staring out of and gave me a slight smile. She had done her job well and she knew it.

After verifying Ms. Cho's story, along with several weeks of follow-up investigation and several more extortion payments, Lieutenant Sampila and I met with the Gang Unit prosecutor's office to fill them in on the information we had developed on this case. The Cook County State's Attorney in charge of Gang Prosecutions at the time was a top-notch female prosecutor named Paula Deoliolo.

After she learned what we had accomplished on this case, Paula said, "You guys did a nice job on this so far, and I'd really like to help you out, but I just don't have the resources to dedicate to this case."

I completely understood Paula's position, but we were disappointed. Her office was prosecuting a shitload of gang murder cases, and all of her prosecutors were overloaded with murder trials and murder trial preparations. The work required to handle a complicated case like this one effectively—on top of all the other important gang investigations her office was tasked with—made it nearly impossible. Paula's Gang Unit prosecutors were handling an unbelievable caseload. The murders just kept piling up, and at times there were several new murders a day.

After discussing our options, Lieutenant Sampila remembered a meeting between the Chicago division of the FBI and the CPD that he had attended several weeks earlier, in which the FBI expressed an interest in working cases in conjunction with the CPD. The FBI supervisor who headed this meeting was a supervisory special agent (SSA) named Grant Ashley. Lieutenant Sampila contacted SSA Ashley and explained the information we had developed during our short investigation. The FBI was immediately interested in the case.

After several meetings and strategy sessions to hammer out a memorandum of understanding (MOU) at the FBI Chicago Division headquarters in the heart of downtown Chicago, the Asian Gang and Organized Crime Task Force was officially formed. Sergeant Hiram Grau, Gang Specialists Pat Walsh, Bob Ditusa, and I were all then officially detailed from the CPD Gang Crimes Unit to the FBI to work in this new elite task force, along with a dedicated squad of FBI agents.

We were sworn in and deputized as special investigators by the U.S. Marshals Service and the FBI, and we were welcomed with open arms into the FBI family. After extensive background checks, we were all given top-secret security clearances. It was a great honor to be issued FBI and U.S. Marshals credentials, which we all carried proudly. But truth be known, the proudest things we carried were still our Chicago

Police gang specialist stars. My wife Gail was happy about my new assignment. She saw it as a promotion and a less dangerous assignment than working undercover in the Gang Unit.

Not long after we were detailed to the FBI, we had a meeting with Deputy Superintendent George Ruckrich, a great cop and an excellent boss. He said, "I want to congratulate you on the work you're doing, but don't forget where you come from!" What Ruckrich meant was: don't embarrass the Chicago Police Department, and always remember that "you're Chicago cops, not FBI agents."

He also said, "I let the FBI know that I was sending over my best guys to work on their task force." What a compliment that was, coming from one of the top cops on the department. It meant a lot to me and my fellow coppers on the task force that Deputy Ruckrich thought so highly of us. We were off on another exciting adventure in all of our careers. The FBI gave me and Sergeants Grau, Walsh, and Ditusa our own desks with plaques that had the FBI logo and Task Force Officer with our individual names. It might seem like a small detail, but very few of the 12,000+ CPD cops had the luxury of having their own desks, especially the fancy large wooden desks we were given. We even had desk drawers that had locks on them. This was quite an upgrade; in the Gang Unit, forty gang specialists shared five cheap metal desks—the type used car salesmen have.

To sweeten the deal further, we now had leased cars that were assigned to us 24/7. Other great perks included undercover identification and credit cards for gas and other expenses we would need to pay for as we conducted our investigations. To say we were blessed to have this assignment would be an understatement.

Once the red tape and the general logistics of our new task force were squared away, it was time to get down to some serious police work. We started fast right out of the gate by gathering intelligence, such as photos, addresses, cars, and license plate numbers on the crew extorting Ms. Cho. We also had the FBI tech squad install hidden microphones and tiny pinhole cameras in various locations of her nightclub. We even rented a vacant dental office located directly across the street from the club entrance; it served as an ideal location from which to videotape the front entrance to her place. We referred to the vacant office as our "perch." The FBI tech squad installed monitors for the hidden cameras in our perch so we could observe what our hidden cameras and microphones were recording.

≈≈≈≈≈

As they say, timing is everything. Once the task force was up and running, crime in the various Asian communities experienced a major spike. There were a rash of restaurant robberies and home invasions, occurring mainly in the Korean community on the north side of the city. Chicago is a diverse city. Many ethnic groups have carved out parts of the city as their own. In some areas of Chicago you would think you were in a foreign country. For example, Lawrence Avenue is also known as "Seoul Boulevard" due to the many Koreans in that neighborhood. Chicago also has the largest concentrated Polish population outside of Poland. Driving down Belmont Avenue, you would think you were in a city in Poland by the storefront signs. The same is true for 26th Street on the south side of the city—you would swear you were in a city in the heart of Mexico. These are just a few of the many examples of Chicago's varied and culturally diverse neighborhoods.

With the increase in crime and the many types of violent crimes being committed in many of the Asian communities in the city, the news coverage was intense. Armed robberies of Asian restaurants and violent home invasions of Asian businessmen by masked gunmen were occurring at an alarming rate. Our task force was directed by the CPD bosses to get involved in investigating them, as well as monitoring Ms. Cho's nightclub. The Korean community was hit particularly hard by the increase in very violent crimes. At one point, the Chicago Korean Businessmen's Association talked about hiring armed vigilantes to patrol and protect the Korean community along Lawrence Avenue.

Our new task force hit the streets hard. We thoroughly investigated all the armed robberies and violent home invasions that were reported to the police. We even heard about a few robberies that weren't reported to the police. As we worked the street in Chinatown, Koreatown, and Little Saigon (Chicago's Vietnamese community, located near Argyle Street), we started making progress in identifying and gathering critical information on some of the bad guys involved in these robberies. We also began to develop informants in the various Asian communities who provided us critical information that had a major impact on our task force's effectiveness in solving some significant cases.

Our strong street presence sealed our reputation as a new force to fight Asian crime, and we became well-known. People started to reach out to us and provide information about the local criminals. The Asian Gang and Organized Crime Task Force was about to change the atmosphere in all the Asian communities throughout the city. My partners and I let everyone in Chinatown, Koreatown, and Little Saigon know that we meant business. The honest hardworking people finally had help in making their communities safe from the rampant crime and intimidation that had been plaguing their communities. We used street stops and informants to identify the gang members causing the most problems. Just like we did in the Gang Unit, after we identified the bad guys, we worked hard to make their lives miserable. Success didn't happen overnight, but we did make some good arrests.

In 1990, after I'd known Ms. Cho for a while, she asked me, "Are you interested in meeting a friend of mine who needs some help?" As we got further along in the conversation about her friend, she finally said, "I'm uncomfortable having this conversation with you because she runs a massage parlor that only caters to Asian customers, and I don't know how you feel about that."

I answered, "Ms. Cho, you know I've always told you that if you know of anyone else who would be interested in talking to me, please let me know. I'd be happy to talk to your friend."

In the real world of police work, the truth is that you don't go to a church group to develop street sources and informants. The best informants a cop can have are the ones who already have a pipeline into criminal activity.

So a meeting was set for me to meet her and her friend. I was very interested in meeting this woman, because her massage parlor/whorehouse was exactly the kind of place to find the bad guys we were looking for. At the first meeting we were supposed to have, Ms. Cho's friend got cold feet at the last minute and chickened out. Ms. Cho and I met anyway and she said, "I am so sorry she did not show. I think she is still afraid."

I reassured her, "Ms. Cho, please tell your friend that she won't have any problems with me."

She continued, "My friend's massage parlor is run out of a large three-bedroom apartment—it's not a typical storefront massage parlor that is commonly seen in cities and towns all across the country." Ms. Cho never gave me the location but explained, "My friend's business isn't a real massage parlor; it is a place of prostitution." I had already figured that out, but once I learned the place was run out of an apartment, I knew exactly what time it was.

I wanted to develop this woman as a source to catch bigger fish, not to arrest her for running a whorehouse. I reassured Ms. Cho, "I understand the situation, and I'm very interested in meeting your friend. If she is willing to cooperate with me, I'll do my best to help her out in any way I can."

We set up another meeting, and Ms. Cho's friend showed up this time. We met at a Jewish deli on the city's north side. When I entered the deli, I spotted Ms. Cho and her friend sitting at a booth. I walked over to greet them, and Ms. Cho got up to give me a hug. She then sat back down next to her friend as I slid into the booth across from them and said, "Pat, I'd like you to meet my very good friend."

I reached out my hand and said, "Hi, and thank you so much for meeting with me."

As we shook hands, Ms. Cho's friend said, "Hello, I'm Ms.

Kay."

Ms. Kay was extremely nervous and had a hard time making eye contact with me. She also kept her hand up covering most of her face. She didn't look anything like I had expected: a bit younger that Ms. Cho, maybe in her mid thirties and quite plain. I don't think anyone would ever guess that Ms. Kay ran whores for a living; she looked much more like a typical Asian housewife.

I immediately went to work to convince her that I had no interest in what she did for a living: "Ms. Kay, I want to solve the robberies and other violent crimes that are occurring in the Asian communities spread throughout Chicago. You can help, and we can help you in return."

Ms. Cho also tried to calm Ms. Kay's fears: "Pat is my very good friend. One hundred percent you can trust him."

Eventually, Ms. Kay seemed to calm down and relax a little. I gave her my business card and pager number and said, "Please call me anytime, Ms. Kay. I look forward to being your friend."

Chapter 21

WITH MS. KAY'S HELP

I left my first meeting with Ms. Kay unsure if I would ever see her again. However, it wasn't too long before my life would revolve around her, her massage parlor, and the information it and the girls who plied their trade there generated for me. Little did I know at the time, but this meeting was the beginning of a multi-year relationship that would take me to many cities around the country and result in seven trips to Toronto, Canada. I also traveled to different cities, following up on information directly provided by Ms. Kay. I took many of these trips with her accompanying me as my CI.

It took several other meetings with both Ms. Cho and Ms. Kay to gain her trust, just as I had gained Ms. Cho's. As with all areas of police work, informants are a key component to solving most crimes. The Asian Gang and Organized Crime Task Force now had two secret weapons, Ms. Cho and Ms. Kay.

My squad and I really started to concentrate on the armed robberies and home invasions based on their inside information about those committing the crimes, not only in Chicago but in many of the suburbs, too. At the time, the Asian gang bangers responsible for most of these crimes operated openly because they'd intimidated entire Asian communities into silence. And like most criminals, they couldn't keep their mouths shut. Almost everyone in law enforcement at the time thought that Asian gangs and Asian organized crime figures were too close-knit and secretive to be infiltrated, but I was bound and determined to change that mindset.

Most of the solid criminal information we were getting came from Ms. Kay's massage parlor. The gang bangers couldn't stay away from the place; the lure of pretty Asian girls drew them there like moths to a bright light. Ms. Kay kept the pretty, young Asian prostitutes busy. She also kept the place stocked with new girls who worked a prostitution circuit set up in Asian communities across the country. The girls would stay at Ms. Kay's for a month or two and then move on to another city to work at another massage parlor. New girls were always coming and going.

Ms. Kay's place was more than a massage parlor: it also functioned as a hangout spot for the gang bangers to drink, smoke, and shoot the shit on her comfortable couches in the living room. Many of these gang bangers would hang out and drink for hours before or after having sex with her girls.

Ms. Kay was a real pro; she would ply these bangers with beer and liquor to get them talking, sometimes even bragging, about the crimes they were committing. My squad mates and I couldn't have planned a better setup. With Ms. Kay's help, we knew the cars these guys drove, their phone numbers, and where they worked and hung out. She was not only extremely valuable as an informant in Chicago; she had contacts all across the country and was connected to Asian crime networks in Toronto, Canada. Through her vast network of contacts and connections from her prostitution business, we were able to make cases that would never have been possible without her help.

I believe that almost all ethnic groups have some form of organized prostitution in their communities. After all, prostitution is often referred to as the world's oldest profession. What made Asian prostitution unique, though, was the fact that Asian prostitutes worked a well-oiled circuit. Many larger cities had female "mama-sans," who ran the prostitution business, watched over the girls, and catered to their needs. They even had travel agents for the girls, who arranged for airline flights between the circuit cities they traveled.

Information was coming at my squad nonstop—not only from

Chicago, but because of Ms. Kay's nationwide network of working girls, we were getting inside information on some pretty serious crimes throughout the United States and Canada. With her help, we were also able to solve cases or get inside information on gambling, loan sharking, murder, and political corruption cases.

Chapter 22

THAI HOOKERS

One of the saddest murder cases I became involved in while assigned to the Asian Task Force took place at 908 Arch Street in Philadelphia's Chinatown. The murder victim was Todd Manga, a twenty-three-year-old security guard. Manga was brutally murdered on August 4, 1995, execution style: three gunshots to the back of his head and one shot to his face.

The day after Todd Manga was shot to death in a massage parlor on Arch Street in Philadelphia, my CI, Ms. Kay, told me that some of the working girls from Philly showed up at her place, talking about seeing a cop getting shot and killed the previous day in Philadelphia's Chinatown. I immediately dropped everything I was doing and set up a meeting with her. This was an important case, if what Ms. Kay told me was true.

When we got together, she said, "The girls told me there was a robbery at a licensed massage parlor on Arch Street. I know the place because the owner is an old friend of mine. A group of Vietnamese gang members have been trying to collect extortion payments from her, but my friend is a tough lady, and she refuses to pay the gang money or to be intimidated by them."

In an effort to outmaneuver the gang, Ms. Kay's friend had apparently hired a security agency to provide a uniformed security guard who would sit inside the front entrance and protect the place.

Ms. Kay added, "My friend thought that this security guard would take care of her gang problems, but it didn't work."

In the early morning hours of August 4, 1995, Todd Manga was shot in the head three times and once in the face and killed when six Vietnamese gang bangers stormed the massage parlor armed with guns. After murdering Todd, the gang members robbed and ransacked the place, tying up customers, taking their drivers licenses, and threatening them if they cooperated with the police. Manga's murder was supposed to warn the female owner to pay extortion money to the gang "or else."

Ms. Kay said, "Pat, after the murder and the gang bangers fled the scene, the Thai prostitutes working there grabbed a few belongings and also left before the police arrived. The girls are all illegally in the United States from Thailand, and they wanted nothing to do with the police. They came here because they know I run a massage parlor that can provide a safe haven, and it's far from the murder in Philadelphia."

I knew I had to meet them to solve the case.

Several days later, I sat at a table in D'Agostino's pizza parlor on Addison Street, just a couple blocks west of Wrigley Field, the home of the Chicago Cubs. I watched the restaurant's front door, intently waiting for the girls to arrive with Ms. Kay, never in a million years thinking I'd be having a beer and pizza party with five Thai prostitutes in my efforts to solve a murder case in Philadelphia. Looking back, I wish this pizza party didn't have to happen, but it was essential for me to get the inside information law enforcement needed to solve Todd Manga's murder. These girls were the only witnesses and we needed their eyewitness testimony to bring the murderers to justice.

I had never met these Thai prostitutes before, but I knew they needed to see me as a friend. I sat there trying to formulate a plan in my mind about how I was going to handle this highly unusual situation. Finally, the door opened and in walked the five Thai hookers, all decked out to the max, wearing short skirts, high heels, and a ton of makeup. I was surprised by how young and beautiful they all were. My informant, Ms. Kay, was like a sheepdog herding a flock of sheep as she smiled and waved at me. She directed the girls to the table where I sat.

Every eye in the place stared at the Thai girls as they walked toward me. I got up and gave my informant a big hug.

I can't begin to imagine what the people in the restaurant were thinking, but it was show time for me: I really had to be on my game tonight if I was going to get the job done. My job was to solve the brutal murder of Todd Manga, who, by all the accounts, was a good kid who had wanted to become a police officer. If I had to buy beer and pizza for Thai hookers, so be it. Todd's family deserved closure and justice for his brutal murder. I was bound and determined to get them that justice, no matter what it took.

Justice for Todd depended on the success of this unusual beer and pizza get together in the shadow of Wrigley Field in Chicago. Sadly, I would eventually meet his parents and brother when I testified in Philadelphia at his murder trial. We were a long way from Todd Manga's murder scene on Arch Street in Philly's Chinatown. We were also a very long way from Thailand.

I had to win the trust of these Thai hookers and convince them to cooperate with the murder investigation. The fact that they were in the country illegally working as prostitutes and spoke very little English was only part of the problem I faced. Ms. Kay started working her magic, after several uncomfortable minutes of telling the girls what a good and trusted friend I was. She even told the girls that I'd saved her life, which was possibly true; more on that a little later.

We ordered a couple pitchers of beer and a couple pizzas. This was an introduction meeting to make the girls feel comfortable. I knew we had to take it slow or the same thing would happen that did in Philly: The girls would flee Chicago and possibly disappear for good.

After downing a few beers and eating some pizza, the girls seemed to relax a little. Ms. Kay was the interpreter for the girls. She told me that they were not only afraid of the murdering gang bangers, but they were just as afraid of the police. They really worried that they were here illegally and would be arrested, put in jail, and eventually deported back to Thailand.

I understood and was worried I'd never see them again or they would refuse to cooperate. Over the course of the next several months, I would have many meetings with the Thai girls. Several of those meetings included two separate teams of Philadelphia police detectives who flew to Chicago to participate in debriefing the Thai girls on what they witnessed the night Todd Manga was killed. With Ms. Kay's help, these briefings and witness interviews went off without a hitch. Once I was able to gain the girls' trust, everything seemed to be going well and we were making progress on identifying Todd's killers.

On their second trip to Chicago, the Philly detectives brought photos of known Vietnamese gang members. As crazy as it might sound, two of the Thai girls had actually dated two of the gang members outside of the massage parlor. They easily picked out the two killers from an array of photos of known Vietnamese gang members. It's probably hard for the average person to comprehend that these two killers were actually dumb enough to commit a senseless murder in the presence of prostitutes who knew them. Asian crime cases were often extremely unusual and unique in many ways.

Many of the Asian crime cases we worked made me think back to when I was a young cop working the ghetto. I was told, "Forget anything that you used to think was normal. You're working in the ghetto now, things are just different."

That same statement had the exact same meaning and impact on me as I worked Asian crime cases. It was a different world altogether. Getting statements and positive identifications of two of the murder suspects was just the beginning of a wild ride we took before getting justice for Todd's family. The Philly detectives returned to Philadelphia and began tracking down these assholes the Thai girls identified as Todd's killers. It was our job on the task force in Chicago to keep these girls in our pocket, so to speak. The Philly coppers did their job and it wasn't long before several suspects were in custody. My squad mates and I had to reassure the Thai girls that they were going to be protected.

It wasn't going to be easy, but these Thai girls were essential to solving this murder case so we had to deliver on our promise to protect and help them. That meant that we had to do some unique things to keep our promise to the girls. The Asian Task Force was very lucky to have a supervisory special agent (SSA) from US Customs and Immigrations assigned to our team. SSA Reggie Bracey was a great guy and a hardworking law enforcement officer. His work on this murder case was not only unique, but also essential. Reggie was able to make a deal with the government whereby the girls were given temporary legal status—as long as they continued to cooperate and agreed to testify in court when Todd Manga's murder case went to trial.

Another crazy thing our team pulled off was that we got clearance from the State of Illinois for the Thai girls to be issued state identification cards. It was arranged for the girls to be fingerprinted and photographed at a state facility located near Joliet, about an hour's drive from Chicago. One of my teammates had the honor of picking the girls up and driving them out to Joliet. To this day, my squad mate and good friend John Howe still brings up his day with the Thai girls. As John tells it, the girls were hung over from drinking too much the night before. He had to pull his car over several times on the way to Joliet so the Thai girls could throw up, while hanging out his car windows.

John finally got the girls to the Illinois State Police building and went through the process of getting them state photo IDs. This building was the same place that once or twice a month undercover cops from all over the state were issued undercover Illinois drivers licenses (under their aliases) to help in their undercover roles. All undercover cops know that having a good set of legit identification on their person during undercover operations can make a difference in their success or failure, possibly even life or death. Once the Thai girls got their state IDs, we were well on our way. We all knew that nothing my squad mates and I did would ever erase the sadness and horror Todd's family had to deal with, but giving Todd's family some closure by putting his killers in prison might offer them a small measure of comfort.

I flew to Philadelphia twice to testify about my involvement in Todd Manga's murder investigation. The trail had many twists and turns before four of Todd's murderers were finally convicted in 1999 and sentenced to life in prison. One of the crazy aspects of this investigation and trial was that our star witnesses, the Thai prostitutes, had gone back to Philly and were working at the same massage parlor where Todd's murder took place. When it was time for the Thai girls to testify at the murder trial, they didn't show up in court.

Two Philly detectives and I had to go to the massage parlor on Arch Street and literally drag their asses out of their beds. They were crying and told us they were too afraid to testify. I had to call Ms. Kay back in Chicago, and have her talk to the girls on the telephone to convince them to do the right thing and testify to what they saw the night Todd was murdered.

I don't know what she said to the girls, but they got dressed and we drove them to the courthouse. They were shaking and crying the whole time. With the help of an interpreter and a Philly prosecutor, they were prepped for their testimony. We had to keep reassuring them that if they told the truth about what happened the night Todd was murdered, they had nothing to fear, which was true; nothing happened to the girls and they were allowed to return to their "jobs."

Chapter 23

A NIGHT WITH PROFESSOR DAYE

Time marched on and so did Asian-related crime. From gang banging to organized crime cases, my squad never had a dull day. We
constantly found new ways of uncovering and solving the complicated
cases that were unfolding—not only in Chicago, but in many other
cities across the country.

During our time on the task force, my partners and I attended
numerous conferences on the unique aspect of Asian crime. There we
met cops from all over the world who also worked Asian-crime cases. I became active with the International Association of Asian Crime
Investigators (IAACI) and was elected as a two-term president of that
organization for the years 1994 and 1995. IAACI is a group for cops,
federal agents, prosecutors, and criminal intelligence analysts involved
in all areas of Asian crime. It was a great honor to be elected to lead
this international association for two terms. As the president of this
association, I met and became very good friends with people from all
over the world.

In 1994, I traveled to China on an eighteen-day trip with a
delegation of international law-enforcement professionals. We toured
five cities in China and held symposiums (training sessions and discussions) with Chinese police officials. On that trip, I also went to Lhasa,
the capital of Tibet, and had meetings with Tibetan law-enforcement
officials to discuss crime issues in both the United States and other
cities around the world.

Professor Doug Daye was one of the people I met and became good friends with as president of the IAACI. Professor Daye was a college professor from Bowling Green State University in Ohio who was in the process of writing a book about culture-related issues and their effect on policing Asian communities. Daye looked as if he could have been plucked right out of central casting to play a professor in a movie: balding; gray hair; circular, wire-rimmed glasses, and preppy clothes.

Professor Doug Daye came to Chicago to do a three-day ride along in the early 1990s to conduct research for his book. He even stayed at my home during the trip. The night before Professor Daye arrived in Chicago, a tough and feared Vietnamese gang leader named Jimmy Choung was shooting pool with some of his fellow gang members at a pool hall on Broadway Avenue, just north of Argyle Street, when a rival gang member ran up and fired several shots through the pool-hall window. One of the shots hit Choung in the head, causing a grave injury that left him clinging to life on a respirator in an intensive care unit.

I thought taking Professor Daye to see Choung in the hospital's intensive care unit would give him a real-life look at what down-and-dirty Asian crime really looked like.

When the professor and I walked into the darkened hospital room, the first thing we heard was the sound of the respirator doing its job, keeping Jimmy alive. Choung looked like a monster: his head was literally twice its normal size, and his eyes looked like purple tennis balls, swollen shut and bulging. I could hear the professor let out a gasp as he recoiled in total shock. He had never seen anything like this before. I completely understood his reaction. Sadly, I had seen people turned into monsters like this many times before. This is how someone looked who had been shot in the head.

The professor and I stayed at Choung's bedside only for a short time, as he was unconscious and in a drug-induced coma. Also, I could see the professor was overwhelmed with emotion and visibility shaken by the sight of Jimmy. I knew almost immediately that it was probably a bad decision on my part to bring the professor to see Jimmy in the condition he was in. I quickly realized that I had to get Professor Daye out of there before he passed out on me.

I leaned over Choung and said, "Hang in there, Jimmy." I gently patted Choung on the shoulder and Professor Daye and I left the room. Even though Jimmy was a gang member and on the other side of the law, I still viewed him as a human being. You have to be a pretty cold person not to have genuinely sad feelings to see someone in Jimmy's state and not feel bad for them. Even though we were on opposite sides of the law, we were just two guys traveling the road of life, each in his own unique way, trying to make the best of our lots in life. Jimmy and I were different, but who's to say that couldn't have been me lying there in a coma and Jimmy the cop who did really care about me?

As we left the hospital, Professor Daye stopped as soon as we were outside the hospital entrance, grabbed my arm, looked me straight in the eye and in a sincere and concerned voice asked, "Pat, how do you deal with crazy things like this?"

I said, "Doug, sometimes I wonder myself. It's a weird thing to describe, but this shit often haunts me more than I want to admit. However, somehow we cops have to learn how to deal with it. I've woken up in the middle of the night many times thinking about the crazy shit I've seen and dealt with but life goes on and I've learned that this is the job I always dreamed of doing and this is part of a cop's life. It can get pretty ugly and hard to deal with at times."

Police officers have a suicide rate that is twice the rate of the general population; some officers get so overwhelmed by the sadness and ugliness they must endure as a cop that the pain becomes too much to handle. Yet we are supposed to deal with this ugliness and sadness without complaint. Police officers are expected to act like robots, never showing our emotions. Any mistakes we make bring severe criticism and intense scrutiny. The fact is that cops are only human and must endure a lifetime of shit most normal citizens couldn't handle.

This was Professor Daye's first night with me. He was supposed to do a three-night ride along. He only lasted two nights. The shooting of gang leader Jimmy Choung had the potential to spark a war among several Asian gangs. It was essential that my partners on the task force and I got to work immediately to solve the case and also to send a message that we were going to make their lives miserable if any retaliation shootings occurred. At the time, we weren't sure if the shooter was a rival gang member or possibly a member of Choung's own gang, settling an internal gang dispute.

The professor didn't realize what he was getting himself into. I think he just expected me to give him a tour of Koreatown, Little Saigon, and Chinatown, not to be part of the hectic pace of an FBI violent crime gang squad, hunting down a gang shooter and trying to prevent a gang war from erupting.

The scope and pace of the work we did in the Asian Task Force often required us to work long hours with little sleep, then go right back at it—especially in a volatile situation like Choung's shooting. My squad hit up every informant we had trying to find out what the word on the street was about why Choung's shooting took place. We also hit every known gang hangout. That included pool halls, coffee shops, nightclubs, and any other places Asian gang bangers were known to frequent.

After two days of rolling hardcore with my squad, Professor Daye said, "Pat, I'm exhausted and I need to get back to Ohio. I don't know how you keep up this insane pace! I admire the job you guys do, and I really enjoyed my time with you and your squad. I learned a lot and appreciated the time we spent together, Pat. Please be safe, and thanks again. This was such an eye-opener for me."

In the early 1990s, Asian gangs were just beginning to get a serious foothold in the various Asian communities throughout Chicago. Having informants was pretty much the only way to get information in these tight-knit communities. I was able to develop many very effective informants whose help in providing inside information was critical to solving some complex cases.

Chapter 24

LET THEM EAT PIGEON

I sat at a table in Three Happiness Restaurant in Chicago's China-town, waiting for the owner, Stanley Leuong, to finish talking to one of his customers. Stanley had greeted me when I first walked into his restaurant: "Hello, Pat. I'll be right with you." He then directed me to a table off to the side and away from the other customers. I was there to pick up a special envelope, the same type of envelope I would pick up once a month for nearly a year afterward.

Stanley was a major Chinese organized crime figure in Chica-go. A few months earlier, I had convinced him that I was a corrupt cop who could be bribed. My squad and I knew that Stanley had three le-gitimate businesses in Chicago's Chinatown: one was an import/export business, another was the Three Happiness Restaurant, and the third was a karate school.

My squad and I had set a trap for Stanley after we learned about a major gambling operation he was running out of his karate school. Informant information said that Stanley ran his karate school during the day, but at night he transformed the school into a full-blown gambling casino. Stanley catered only to Asian gamblers and featured *pai gow*, which is a form of double-handed poker, and other gambling games played mainly by Asian gamblers.

Several sources told us that Stanley was looking for a corrupt cop he could pay to warn him if any raids were going to be conduct-ed at his gambling operation. We started planting information on the street that I was corrupt and willing to take money to overlook certain types of criminal activity. We used Ms. Kay and her prostitution operation as one of the ways to convince Stanley that I was protecting her illegal brothel. With her help, Stanley bought into the fact that I was approachable and just might be the guy he was looking for to protect his gambling operation.

I received a call one day from an unknown male who said, "Mr. Leoung is interested in talking to you about a possible business proposition."

I said, "Sure. I'd be happy to meet with Stanley."

"Tell me where and when, and I will inform Mr. Leung."

"How about at the Harris Restaurant on Irving Park Road, just east of Kedzie Avenue? You tell me what day and what time, and I'll be there."

"I'll check with Stanley and get back to you."

"Great! Tell Stanley I look forward to meeting him."

I couldn't wait to tell my squad mates about the call I received. I immediately called my partner Pat Walsh: "Hey, some guy called me and told me Stanley wants to meet with me about a business proposition."

"Perfect, we're in!" he said with glee.

Walsh and I met up and immediately headed downtown to the FBI headquarters building where our office was located. We had a squad meeting and started to plan how to handle my upcoming meeting. We contacted the FBI tech squad and arranged to wire me for my meeting with Stanley. My squad would cover the meeting in a nearby covert van.

The next day the same guy called me and asked, "Can you meet with Stanley at seven o'clock tonight?"

I answered, "Tonight would be great. I'll be there at seven. Does Stanley know where the Harris Restaurant is?"

The caller said, "Yes, he knows where it is, and he'll see you at seven."

I was both nervous and excited. It seemed inevitable now that Stanley was on the hook; I just had to slowly reel him in.

My squad and I met at a parking garage near the Harris Restaurant, and an FBI wire was taped to my body. Two tiny microphones were taped to my chest with wires taped to my rib cage that were attached to a small metal recorder secured to the middle of my back. I tried to stay focused because I was almost certain Stanley was going to ask me to protect his gambling operation.

I got to the restaurant early, grabbed a booth, and waited for Stanley to show up. About 7:05 p.m., in walked Stanley, but he wasn't alone. He was with a guy who looked to be around forty. I gave Stanley a wave as he scanned the restaurant looking for me. Stanley and the other guy I didn't recognize approached me and both slid into the booth across from me. Stanley shook my hand and introduced me to his friend he called Benny. I shook Benny's hand, saying, "Nice to meet you."

The game was on, and it was funny because I got an instant case of diarrhea of the mouth; I rambled on like a fool. I started telling Stanley and his friend about the restaurant's chocolate éclairs; I went on for several minutes about how big they were and how thick the chocolate on top of them was. My buddies outside were listening to me drone on about the éclairs, laughing their asses off. Later, one said, "For Christ's sake, you sounded like an éclair salesman, not an undercover cop trying to hook up a Chinese organized crime figure."

I was probably more nervous than I should have been; after all, I was used to dealing with hardened street gang members when I worked undercover, not older Chinese guys. Even though Stanley and his friend knew I was a cop, it took some time to calm my nerves.

I eventually got down to business and asked, "So how can I help you, Stanley?"

He seemed anxious as he replied, "You know about my business by the karate school right?"

"Yes, I've heard about your gambling operation; how's it going?"

"It's fine, but I might need your help."

"I can make sure you won't have any trouble with the police, if that's what you're looking for here."

Stanley gave me a big smile and then said, "Your protection of my place will be of great importance to me. I'm happy to pay for your protection services."

"Well, I'll have to involve a few other people to protect you the right way."

"I understand. I can pay you $2,000 a month."

"That should work out fine because, like I said, I have to share this money with some other people."

He seemed happy but then asked, "So how will this work?"

I answered, "If you give me your cell number, I will call you in advance of any pending raids on your gambling business, so you have time to close it down before the police show up." To sweeten the sting on Stanley I added, "My friend works in the vice control office, and no cop can do a raid without getting a raid number. My friend will know if any cop requests a raid on your gambling business at the karate school."

Stanley and I agreed that we would meet once a month so he could pay me the $2,000 protection money. I would come to his Three Happiness Restaurant in Chinatown to collect the monthly payments. This meeting with Stanley and his friend would be the start of a year-long case before we finally decided to take Stanley down on bribery and gambling charges. We had high hopes of turning him into a major organized crime informant.

I browsed the menu, looking for something to order. I always ordered food when I met with Stanley at his restaurant. As I waited for him, a male waiter brought me a cup of hot tea. I was a little nervous about the FBI wire I was wearing. Stanley had never searched me before, but in the crazy world of cops and robbers, "never before" meant nothing. All cops know that if you get too comfortable or complacent, you could get yourself killed, especially when working undercover on a Chinese organized crime case.

After a few minutes, Stanley walked over to my table and sat down. He seemed nervous, but then every time I met with him, he seemed nervous. He and I knew the stakes were high in the game we were playing. As always, he said, "Pat, have some food. You have time to eat, don't you?"

I knew my partners on the Asian Task Force were parked in a nearby van, listening to the wire I wore and recording every word.

I wanted to fuck with my partners' minds a little bit, so I asked Stanley, "How's the pigeon? I've never had that before." Unbelievably, the menu had pigeon, and the dish was really called "Pigeon," not some other fancy name, but fuckin' pigeon. I was born and raised in Chicago, and I've never met anyone who had ever eaten fucking pigeon. In Chicago, pigeons are frequently called flying rats.

Stanley said, "It's very good, Pat." He then added with a smile, "You know all my food is good. Try the pigeon."

"All right then, I'll have an order of the pigeon and an egg roll."

My partners in the van couldn't believe I had just ordered a pigeon dinner. I was laughing on the inside, because I knew I'd just mind-fucked my buddies who were listening in the van. To tell the truth, the pigeon didn't taste too bad. I know I'll never eat a pigeon again, but there's a lot of crazy shit I did as a cop that I would never even think of doing again. I have always believed that life is a very interesting game, and I'll be the first to admit that I enjoyed playing the game on the edge sometimes.

I knew this was going to be my last meeting with Stanley at his restaurant; my squad was making plans for Stanley's arrest, which would take place in a few days if things went as planned.

The plan was for me to call Stanley and tell him that I had to meet him as soon as possible to discuss an important issue. When I called, Stanley asked, "What's wrong, Pat? Is everything okay?"

I said, "Everything is fine. I just need to talk with you, but I don't want to talk on the telephone. In fact, I have some good news to discuss with you. I work a side job as security at the downtown Chicago Holiday Inn. I'm working tomorrow night; do you think you could stop by for a short talk?"

Stanley said, "Sure I can. Where is this hotel?"

I told him, "It's at 350 N. Orleans. I can meet you in the lobby, which is on the fifteenth floor. I start work at 6:00 p.m., so can we meet around 7:00 p.m.?"

Without hesitation, Stanley said, "I'll meet you there tomorrow at seven, Pat."

"Great, Stanley. I'll see you then."

I really did work part-time security at this hotel as a side job, but I would be on special duty tomorrow when I met Stanley. I arranged to have two adjoining rooms available for my final meeting with Stanley. As I waited for Stanley, my squad mates were upstairs preparing for his arrest. My job was to bring Stanley up to one of the rooms for a brief conversation, then several cops and FBI agents would enter from the adjoining room and give Stanley the bad news that would change his life forever.

I sat there waiting anxiously in the hotel lobby for Stanley to arrive. The lobby was large and had several seating areas arranged with chairs, couches, and cocktail tables. As I sat there, I couldn't help but think about what had gone on over the past year and how Stanley would react when he would be taken into custody. Stanley was about seventy years old, and after almost a year of meeting and dining with him once a month, I felt a little guilty about what was going to happen to him. Don't get me wrong: Stanley was a criminal, but he did have a wife and kids, and I kept thinking how the illegal shit he was involved in would affect not only Stanley but also his family. I placed those disturbing thoughts into the trash heap in my mind, the same place I had also stored away the many other disturbing things I did and experienced in my career as a Chicago cop.

I was seated as close to the hotel elevators as possible to spot Stanley as soon as he got off the elevator. I didn't have to wait long; a few minutes after seven, Stanley stepped off the elevator.

I walked up to him, shook hands, and said "I'm glad you could make it."

Stanley responded, "I'm happy to, Pat. Is everything okay?"

"Sure, Stanley, everything is great. I just have an idea I wanted to talk to you about. Let's go upstairs; I have a room where we can talk in private."

Stanley and I got back on the elevator and headed up to a room on the eighteenth floor. I was happy that it was a short ride, because I was feeling nervous about what was about to happen.

As soon as we entered the hotel room, I said, "This is going to be a great night." That was the code phrase to signal the arrest team to move in. Suddenly, the connecting door to the adjoining room burst open and several cops and FBI agents ran into the room with guns drawn, shouting, "FBI! You're under arrest." Stanley stood there frozen like a statue. He was immediately searched for weapons as I was being ushered out of the room.

My FBI supervisor had decided that I should not be involved in Stanley's interrogation, which took place in the same room he was arrested. The plan was to try and flip him and get him to help us ensnare other Chinese organized crime figures. The FBI had obtained numerous photos of the important things in Stanley's life as leverage. For example, they had photos of his wife, kids, and his home to let him realize what he was about to lose. With the case we had on him, he was looking at some serious jail time. The FBI interrogators only worked on him for a couple of hours. To my complete surprise, they let him go, telling him, "Sleep on your future tonight and contact us tomorrow."

To say I was stunned to hear that they let Stanley go would be a huge understatement. It made no sense to me, but the FBI interrogators thought he was willing to cooperate and turn informant, so they were comfortable giving Stanley a break until the next day. This was one of the dumbest moves I had seen in my eleven years working with the FBI; I just couldn't believe it. Stanley should have been locked up that night in the Metropolitan Correctional Center in downtown Chicago to see what his future would be like if he didn't cooperate.

I wasn't at all surprised when Stanley didn't contact the FBI interrogating agents the next day. Word on the street was that Stanley had immediately fled the country to some unknown location and hadn't been seen since that night at the hotel. Even a rookie agent would have known that, at the very least, they should have seized Stanley's passport so he couldn't leave the country. A year's worth of work by me and my squad, turned out to be for nothing: just another strange twist in the often crazy world of cops and bad guys.

Chapter 25

ANDREW AND ROBERT

He probably never saw it coming. I'm sure Robert never thought Andrew could ever kill anyone in a million years, especially someone who was as good to him as Robert had been. Robert O'Dubaine's life was over in an instant on September 25, 1993. Two gunshots to the head was how Robert met his maker. If he wasn't dead before he hit the cold concrete floor, he died immediately after falling—in a pool of blood in his own garage, right behind his house on North Hermitage Avenue on Chicago's near-north side.

Robert O'Dubaine's murder was set up by Andrew Suh's sister Catherine, who was engaged to marry Robert; they rehabbed homes and owned a nightclub together in Glenview, an upscale Chicago suburb. Both Catherine and Robert had lovers on the side. If it weren't for a crazy set of circumstances, good luck, and call waiting, Andrew and Catherine Suh would not be in prison today. Andrew received 100 years in prison for Robert's murder. Catherine was sentenced to natural life without the possibility of parole. She was also suspected of killing her mother in 1987 by stabbing her thirty-seven times in the neck and head at their family-owned dry cleaners in Evanston, Illinois.

Andrew Suh was the last person you'd ever expect to turn into a cold-blooded killer. By all accounts, he was a good kid, an honor student from a well-respected Korean family. He had been class president while attending Loyola Academy, a prestigious Catholic high school in the upper-class suburb of Wilmette, only a short drive north from the city limits of Chicago. Loyola Academy had many celebrity alumni, including actors Bill Murray and Chris O'Donnell. I can't be certain, but it's probably a good bet that Andrew was the most unlikely killer ever to walk the halls of Loyola Academy.

Our hunt for Andrew lasted for days and had many unusual twists and turns, including a threat to my life. Things got tense until we finally got Andrew Suh off the street. I took no pleasure in arresting Andrew and putting him in jail for 100 years. In all likelihood, Andrew and his sister Catherine will almost certainly die in prison. It still bothers me to this day what Andrew did and what he threatened to do.

I was totally blown away one night during our hunt for Andrew when my informant, Navi, said, "Pat, Andrew said you are one of three people he wants to kill before he goes to prison."

I thought, *Oh sure, another wild exaggeration.* Just some of the same old bravado bullshit talked about on the street. With an incredulous look on my face I said, "Navi, I can't believe this! Andrew is just blowing smoke, bro. I've heard this kind of crap before."

Navi grabbed my arm, looked me straight in the eye, and said, "Pat, this isn't bullshit; it's for real, man. Andrew is straight up crazy. He's completely lost his mind." I still wasn't buying it, but then Navi said something that totally blew me away: "Pat, Andrew has followed you, man. He said he could have already killed you if he wanted to, but he's waiting to do it closer to the court date for his murder case."

That's when it really hit me: this wasn't some bullshit story I was being fed—it was fucking real! This asshole already killed Robert, the guy who had raised him like a son. I knew he would have no problem killing me, too.

I didn't want to scare my wife by calling to warn her about this very real threat on my life. I wanted to get home as fast as I could to make sure my wife, Gail, and my son, Ryan, were safe. I was terrified of what Andrew might do to my family. I kept thinking: *This prick had actually followed me. How did I not spot him? I'm a seasoned street cop, for Christ's sake.*

I still had a hard time believing it. My mind raced: *Could Andrew have followed me home? Does this fucking nut job know where I live?* I quickly made arrangements to meet with Navi again the next day. I needed time to process what I'd learned and formulate a plan to get Andrew locked up and off the street ASAP. I also needed to get home right away.

I blew through every red light between the parking lot where I'd met with Navi and my house. The ride home would normally take about fifteen minutes; I made it home in half that time. I was so relieved when I pulled up in front of my house: everything seemed normal. I raced up my front stairs, my heart pounding violently in my chest. My hands shook as I hurriedly unlocked my front door. I was never so happy to see my wife's beautiful smile when I walked into my living room.

She looked at me, surprised, and asked, "Why are you home so early?" A tremendous relief immediately came over me. Gail knew something was wrong by the way I was acting and added, "Pat, is everything okay?"

I didn't want to worry her, so I just said, "I just have a bad headache. I'm fine." I knew right then that everything would be fine; that rotten prick Andrew's life of freedom was quickly coming to an end. Andrew would be in jail very soon, no ifs, ands, or buts about it. My squad made an all-out effort and tracked Andrew down and arrested him the next day on a robbery charge. They got his bond revoked, and he's been locked up in prison ever since. Catherine had fled to Hawaii but was apprehended a short time later.

Chapter 26

Harry Mook

My informant, Ms. Kay, FBI agent Dan Bellich, and I had flown to Boston to ensnare Harry Mook (aka Goon Chun Yee), who was a major figure in Boston's Chinese organized crime community and the past president of *Hung Mun* (Chinese Freemasons Association). Several weeks prior to this trip, Ms. Kay had told me she was very close to Harry Mook, who she called "Mookie." She went on to tell me, "I can help you get him, Pat. He is a really big gangster."

After checking with the Boston FBI, I learned Mook was a major target in Boston's Chinese organized crime network. He was involved in many aspects of crime—not only the prostitution business, but also loan sharking, gambling, money laundering, and public corruption. The plan was to lure Mook to Ms. Kay's hotel room, which would be wired, to record their discussions about how to move Asian hookers to various cities throughout the United States.

I was sound asleep in a Boston hotel room, tired after the morning flight from Chicago and several meetings with FBI agents and a special squad of Boston cops. The pounding on my hotel room door startled me awake. I glanced at the clock radio on the nightstand next to the bed and saw it was 2:30 a.m. Wearing only my underwear and wondering who the hell was frantically banging on my door at this late hour, I got out of bed, looked through the peephole, and saw Ms. Kay with another Asian female who was obviously a prostitute.

I quickly opened the door to let them in. The woman with Ms. Kay was sobbing, holding a hand over her mouth, and wearing only a towel. I stood there wearing only multicolored bikini underwear and thought, *Could this scene get any weirder?* All kinds of crazy shit ran through my head at this point. It was hard to wrap my mind around what could possibly be happening as I hurriedly ushered Ms. Kay and the other Asian woman into my hotel room. *Would Harry Mook show up at my door any minute?*

I asked Ms. Kay point-blank, "What the fuck is going on here?" as I nervously peered through the peephole again.

The Asian hooker stood there sobbing softly as Ms. Kay said, "Mookie came to the hotel earlier tonight drunk and looking for sex with one of my girls." Unbeknownst to me, my CI had set Mook up with the hooker now crying in my hotel room.

Ms. Kay continued, "Well, he got pissed off over something she said and punched her right in the mouth. Then he got dressed in a hurry and left the hotel before security or the police could come. We didn't know what to do, so we ran down the hall to your room, Pat. I'm sorry, but we're scared!" It looked like our well-orchestrated plan was about to turn to shit.

As my CI was telling me what happened, and before I could even put my pants on, there was another knock on my door. I looked through the peephole and saw two white guys standing outside my room. At least it wasn't Harry Mook, but I also knew it wasn't good. I opened the door and one guy said, "I'm the hotel manager on duty, and you have to leave the hotel immediately."

I said, "Please give me a minute to get dressed."

As I closed the door, I told Ms. Kay, "You two just sit on the bed. I'll be right back."

I put on my pants and a shirt, then went out into the hallway, and told the two guys: "I'm going to tell you something, and you better understand I'm not bullshitting: I'm with the FBI, and I'm working a very sensitive investigation." I showed them my FBI credentials and warned them in a whisper, "If you tell anyone about anything that just happened, you will both be arrested and charged with interfering with a federal investigation. Do you understand me?"

The looks on their faces were priceless as they nodded and said, "Yes, sir!" They walked away in shock.

I had to knock softly on the door to get back in my room. Ms. Kay opened the door with a sad look on her face. She knew she had screwed up and that I wasn't happy about what was happening. I whispered to her, "Take that poor girl into the bathroom and tell her everything is okay. Tell her I'm your boyfriend. Now go get this girl some clothes and hurry back here immediately!"

As the Asian prostitute sat in my bathroom still sobbing, I paced my hotel room and wondered what to do next as I kept checking the peephole, not knowing what else to expect.

Ms. Kay was back in a flash, tapping on my door. I let her in and said, "Give the girl the clothes and tell her to get dressed. You come back out and talk to me." I was still in shock and wondered if I should wake up my partner, FBI Agent Dan Bellich, who was with me on this trip and sleeping soundly in his room just down the hall. I needed time to think this through.

I told Ms. Kay, "Now take this girl back to your room in case Mookie returns. And make sure she thinks that I'm your boyfriend. I hope you didn't tell her who I really am!"

Ms. Kay said, "She doesn't know anything, and I can convince her you're my boyfriend."

I said, "Good! Call me if anything else happens tonight. If everything is okay, call me in the morning when you get up."

After Ms. Kay and the prostitute left my room, I sat on the bed trying to come up with my next move. I made the decision not to wake up Agent Bellich. What good would that do? Mook had already left the hotel, and it was highly unlikely he would return. Exhausted, I got undressed and tried to fall back asleep again.

When I awoke the next morning, I called Dan Bellich's room

and said, "We need to talk right away. Do you want to come to my room or should I come by you?"

Dan kept asking, "What's up? I need to know what's going on."

I didn't feel comfortable talking on the hotel phone, so I said, "I'll get ready and be right over. I'll explain it all to you in a few minutes."

I quickly got dressed and headed to Bellich's room to fill him in on what went on overnight. Dan just kept shaking his head as I told him what happened. We decided to talk to Ms. Kay and try to salvage our original plan to get Mookie on tape talking about illegal prostitution activities.

I contacted Ms. Kay and said, "Meet me and Agent Bellich in about an hour in our special room. We'll be waiting there for you."

She asked, "Will any Boston cops be there?"

"No, it will be just Dan and me. We need your help to keep things on track."

Our "special room" was actually a suite in the hotel that we had rented to hold meetings with our law enforcement colleagues from Boston to plan our strategy in the investigation of Harry Mook. Ms. Kay showed up about an hour later and Agent Bellich and I had a heart-to-heart talk with her.

I asked, "Ms. Kay, why would you have Mookie come to the hotel without telling us?"

She said, "Mookie called me late last night and wanted a girl for sex, so I called a girl I know and set him up with her. If I didn't do it, he would know that something was wrong. I know I screwed up, and I have a bad feeling about moving forward to get Mookie." She was a superstitious person and kept saying, "This is not good. I don't feel like I want to go through with this anymore. I don't want to deal with any Boston cops or FBI agents. Mookie is a very powerful gangster. He knows a lot of police, and it could be bad for me."

I tried to reassure her that I thought the plan could still work, but she wasn't buying it. I sent her back to her room and said, "I'll call you in a few hours, and don't worry, Ms. Kay. I won't ask you to do anything you're not comfortable with."

It was with regret that I called an emergency meeting with my Boston counterparts to inform them about Mookie and the Asian hooker and the shit that happened overnight. I also had to say, "My CI's got cold feet now and doesn't want to go through with it."

We all parted company awkwardly. I couldn't help but think that if last night hadn't happened, the plan to lure Mookie to Ms. Kay's hotel room and get incriminating statements would have worked. Agent Bellich, Ms. Kay, and I flew home later that night, feeling exhausted and somewhat defeated.

As it turned out, the Boston federal agents from the FBI, US Customs Services, and Immigration and Naturalization Services already had a rock-solid case on Mook. Ms. Kay recording Mookie would have just put a cherry on top of what they had already developed on him. Ultimately, Mook pled guilty to several federal violations and received a forty-six-month sentence in federal prison.

Chapter 27

THE END OF A CAREER

December 31, 1999, was a crazy time throughout the world. The Internet and news outlets across the globe were stoking the fears of what might happen when the clock struck midnight on January 1, 2000. There was a lot of talk of a complete meltdown of the worldwide Internet commerce and all banking systems. The conspiracy theorists had a field day with speculation about what might happen; many so-called experts predicted an apocalypse. Everybody on the planet was uncertain of what might occur when the new millennium hit. All the federal, local, and state agencies were on edge, including my squad in the FBI.

Chicago's mayor at the time, Richard J. Daley, was hosting an international party at McCormick Place, which is a major convention venue located just south of downtown Chicago. Mayor Daley had invited dignitaries from all over the world to celebrate the coming new millennium in Chicago. I was part of a special group of cops and FBI agents assigned to protection duty for these heads of state. I remember walking around McCormick Place with a good friend and fellow gang specialist named Eddy Wiora.

Eddy and I were just shooting the shit about the job of a cop, like many cops do when they get together. We talked about all the crazy things we both experienced while working in the gang unit—all the murders and shootings we worked on and solved. Eddy also said, "Here we are, Pat, all these years later, being bodyguards at a New Year's

Eve party for a bunch of politicians. You know most people wouldn't believe half the shit we've done and experienced! Remember when we put those burglar bars on Ms. Kay's whorehouse after that robbery?"

We both laughed at that one and I kiddingly said, "No shit, maybe we should write a book, Eddy!"

Out of nowhere he said, "Pat, I'm going to pull the pin in March."

"Pulling the pin" is a slang term in the police department for retiring from the job.

I remember being shocked and asking, "Are you sure you're ready to go?"

Without hesitation, Eddy said, "Yeah, Pat, I am. I'm going to leave while I'm still young enough to run my own business and build it up for my three boys. I'm putting my papers in and retiring on March 1." Eddy was one of the hardest working guys I had ever met. He owned his own remodeling business, besides being a dedicated cop.

I said, "I'll believe it when I see it, Ed."

"Pat, I'm not bullshitting you here: March 1 and I'm gone."

The rest of the night the thought of retirement crept into my mind, and each time it did, I quickly perished it. I kept thinking about what life would be like not being a cop—just the thought of it terrified me.

I didn't think about it much over the next several months. Occasionally, the idea of moving on to a new chapter in my life crept back into my mind. I thought about all the crazy shit I did throughout my career, taking many risks that most people would think bordered on crazy, but I kept telling myself, *It's too early. I'm still a young guy.*

Seriously retiring from the force began as just a wild, crazy thought hidden in the deep recesses of my mind. I have to admit, though, that I had actually daydreamed about it a few times before, always dismissing the idea as too insane to actually consider. I had gone to many cops' retirement parties in my career. To me, they always seemed like sad occasions. Every cop looks forward to the day when they can hang it up and go back to the "normal" world. My world for the past twenty-plus years wasn't normal by any standard. I remember one cop at a retirement party I attended saying, "You'll know when it's your time to go. You'll just know."

Then, one day while working surveillance on a Title III federal wiretap case on a Latin King gang member, I was throwing around a football in a parking lot on the shores of Lake Michigan with some squad mates. The Title III means that a federal judge gave my FBI squad permission to tap a suspect's phone calls to help build a criminal case against him and his drug organization. We were just killing time, waiting for our target to hit the street and deliver cocaine and heroin to his customers.

Once our target got rolling, we would follow him to his drug drops and document the delivery that one of the agents in the wire room heard during his phone-call monitoring of the suspect. We would then expand our investigation to include wiretapping the people the suspect had delivered drugs to. Working a wiretap case usually involves long boring hours with nothing exciting happening. Then suddenly, the shit would hit the fan, and we would be scrambling balls to the wall to conduct surveillance and follow our gang target.

The unique aspect of working a Title III was that once the wire was active, the target's calls were being monitored 24/7, so someone was always working. One Sunday morning, we were killing time until something happened on the wire, tossing a football around, when one of the agents got an urgent call from the wire room. He'd overheard our target discussing a possible hit on a rival gang with a fellow gang member. We went literally from having a nice day in the park to racing several miles away to prevent a possible gang hit. As my squad and I prowled the neighborhood, looking for the shooter, I was focused but also started to think about what might possibly happen on this nice Sunday morning: I could get myself killed trying to stop a potential gang murder. As it turned out, the wire room picked up another call indicating the shooting had been called off.

We all went back to the lakefront parking lot and resumed our game of catch with the football. Strange thoughts of possibly leaving the job started to creep back into my mind. I thought of my buddy, Eddy, running his own remodeling business, living a "normal life" and building a future for his three boys.

I've often heard cops talk about it, but I was certain it would never happen to me. I was a Chicago cop through and through: tough as nails. I thought for sure I would go the distance and not retire until I was forced to at the mandatory retirement age of sixty-three. I was only forty-eight when I did something I never in my wildest dreams thought I could do. I had always known this time would come some-day, but I never imagined it would be this early in my life.

On July 1, 2000, I said a sad and emotional goodbye forever to a very close family, a family that I had spent over twenty-six years with. I left this family to start a new life—a new direction I felt I was being drawn into. It was a family that I loved deeply and trusted with my life. It was a very large and caring family that for over twenty-six exciting years I had shared blood, sweat, and many tears with in so many crazy and unusual situations.

As I drove away from the Chicago Police Department's head-quarters building, located at 35th Street and South Michigan Avenue, I felt like I was driving through a foggy haze. My mind was completely numb at the thought of what I had just done. I was scared, sad, and confused. *Had I made the right decision? Was I making a big mistake like many of my closest friends had warned me I was doing?* After the best and most exciting years of my life, it finally hit me that it was really over: I was no longer an active Chicago street cop. My emotions began to flow uncontrollably. It started out slowly as warm tears began welling up in my eyes. I tried to stay focused and kept telling myself this was the right decision to make for me and my family.

I had just filed my official papers to retire from the CPD and I knew that this would be an emotional day for me, but I was surprised at how quickly the deep sadness hit me. I felt physically weak, nauseated, and very much alone as my mind processed what had just taken place in my life. I was a grown man, for Christ's sake, a tough big-city cop, but my emotions still overtook me. I could no longer safely drive, so I pulled over and parked my car.

My mind raced a thousand miles an hour as I sat there realizing that I had just turned in my gang specialist Chicago Police badge that I had carried for many years with great honor, pride, and dedication.

I was about to move into a new phase of my life. When I really thought about it, though, I realized that I wasn't leaving police work forever; I was just taking on a different assignment. I was now going to have the honor and privilege to continue on my path in law enforcement as a professional law-enforcement trainer. It would prove to be a job I would cherish as I shared the experiences and lessons learned (both good and bad) that I was lucky enough to have lived through with my fellow brothers and sisters who proudly and bravely serve their communities throughout the country. I was going to help both young and older officers and federal agents become safer and more effective as they faced the very real challenges of being a law enforcement professional in cities and towns all across this country. I have been doing this for the past fifteen years and still love it, even though I miss being a Chicago street cop every day.

ACKNOWLEDGMENTS

I would like to give special thanks to my wife Gail, my assistant Natalie Walsh, and my editors Jill Welsh and Kim Bookless. Also Pat Walsh and all my partners and the brave men and women of the CPD and the FBI; they have always been family to me and always will be. God Bless and Stay Safe.

ABOUT THE AUTHOR

Pat McCarthy served as a member of the Chicago Police Department for twenty-six years, eleven of which were spent on three separate FBI task forces while still employed by the Chicago Police Department. Prior to that, he was an undercover cop in the CPD Gang Crimes Unit, and he was a SWAT team member in Special Operations for six years; three of those years were spent as a sniper/sharpshooter.

Shortly before Mr. McCarthy retired from the police force in 2000, he created a three-day police-training seminar called Street Crimes. Information on the seminar can be viewed at www.StreetCrimes.com. Pat McCarthy has also been a professional public speaker for the past twenty years, lecturing throughout North America and abroad about developing informants, interview techniques, surveillance, interrogation techniques, and many other issues related to gang and drug investigations. He is currently working on his second book, titled *Chicago Gang Cops*.

He still lives in the north side of Chicago with his wife, Gail. Their son, Ryan, has carried on the family tradition by becoming an officer in the Chicago Police Department in 2009.